Standards Practice Book

Houghton
Mifflin
Harcourt

For Home or School

Grade 1

INCLUDES:
- Home or School Practice
- Lesson Practice and Test Preparation
- English and Spanish School-Home Letters
- Getting Ready for Grade 2 Lessons

CRITICAL AREA

Operations and Algebraic Thinking

COMMON CORE **Critical Area** Developing understanding of addition, subtraction, and strategies for addition and subtraction within 20

1 Addition Concepts

Domain Operations and Algebraic Thinking
Common Core Standards 1.OA.1, 1.OA.3, 1.OA.6

2 Subtraction Concepts

Domain Operations and Algebraic Thinking
Common Core Standards 1.OA.1, 1.OA.6, 1.OA.8

3 Addition Strategies

Domain Operations and Algebraic Thinking
Common Core Standards 1.OA.2, 1.OA.3, 1.OA.5, 1.OA.6

4 Subtraction Strategies

Domain Operations and Algebraic Thinking
Common Core Standards 1.OA.1, 1.OA.4, 1.OA.5, 1.OA.6

5 Addition and Subtraction Relationships

Domain Operations and Algebraic Thinking
Common Core Standards 1.OA.1, 1.OA.6, 1.OA.7, 1.OA.8

 **CRITICAL AREA**

Number and Operations in Base Ten

 COMMON CORE **Critical Area** Developing understanding of whole number relationships and place value, including grouping in tens and ones

6 Count and Model Numbers

Domain Number and Operations in Base Ten
Common Core Standards 1.NBT.1, 1.NBT.2, 1.NBT.2a, 1.NBT.2b, 1.NBT.2c, 1.NBT.3

7 Compare Numbers

Domain Number and Operations in Base Ten
Common Core Standards 1.NBT.3, 1.NBT.5

8 Two-Digit Addition and Subtraction

Domain Operations and Algebraic Thinking
Number and Operations in Base Ten

Common Core Standards 1.OA.6, 1.NBT.4, 1.NBT.6

CRITICAL AREA Measurement and Data

COMMON CORE | **Critical Area** Developing understanding of linear measurement and measuring lengths as iterating length units

9 Measurement

Domain Measurement and Data
Common Core Standards 1.MD.1, 1.MD.2, 1.MD.3

	School-Home Letter (English)	P157
	School-Home Letter (Spanish)	P158
9.1	**Hands On** • Order Length	P159
9.2	Indirect Measurement	P161
9.3	**Hands On** • Use Nonstandard Units to Measure Length	P163
9.4	**Hands On** • Make a Nonstandard Measuring Tool	P165
9.5	**Problem Solving** • Measure and Compare	P167
9.6	Time to the Hour	P169
9.7	Time to the Half Hour	P171
9.8	Tell Time to the Hour and Half Hour	P173
9.9	Practice Time to the Hour and Half Hour	P175

10 Represent Data

Domain Measurement and Data
Common Core Standards 1.MD.4

	School-Home Letter (English)	P177
	School-Home Letter (Spanish)	P178
10.1	Read Picture Graphs	P179
10.2	**Hands On** • Make Picture Graphs	P181
10.3	Read Bar Graphs	P183
10.4	**Hands On** • Make Bar Graphs	P185
10.5	Read Tally Charts	P187
10.6	**Hands On** • Make Tally Charts	P189
10.7	**Problem Solving** • Represent Data	P191

CRITICAL AREA Geometry

COMMON CORE **Critical Area** Reasoning about attributes of, and composing and decomposing geometric shapes

11 Three-Dimensional Geometry

Domain Geometry
Common Core Standards 1.G.1, 1.G.2

12 Two-Dimensional Geometry

Domain Geometry
Common Core Standards 1.G.1, 1.G.2, 1.G.3

End-of-Year Resources

Getting Ready for Grade 2

These lessons review important skills and prepare you for Grade 2.

School-Home Letter

Dear Family,

My class started Chapter 1 this week. In this chapter, I will learn to add numbers up to ten, to write addition sentences in different ways, and to use pictures to help me add.

Love, _____

Vocabulary

plus (+) part of an addition sentence that means "to add to"

$$\text{plus}$$
$$1 + 3 = 4$$

sum the answer to an addition sentence

$$2 + 4 = ⑥$$

zero a number that means none; if you add zero to any number, the number does not change

$$1 + 0 = 1$$

Home Activity

Use 10 checkers, crayons, or other small objects. Work with your child to show all the ways to make 10. (1 + 9, 6 + 4, and so on.) Together write addition sentences for each way to make ten.

Literature

Look for this book in a library. Ask your child to count how many objects are on each page.

How Many Snails?: A Counting Book
by Paul Giganti. Greenwillow Books, 1994

Carta para la casa

Querida familia:

Mi clase comenzó el Capítulo 1 esta semana. En este capítulo, aprenderé a sumar números hasta diez, cómo escribir oraciones numéricas de suma de distintas maneras y cómo usar ilustraciones para aprender a sumar mejor.

Con cariño, _____

Vocabulario

más (+) parte de una oración numérica de suma que significa "sumar a"

$$\overset{más}{1 + 3} = 4$$

suma la respuesta a una oración numérica de suma

$$2 + 4 = \boxed{6}$$

cero un número que significa nada; si sumas cero a cualquier número, ese número no cambia

$$1 + 0 = 1$$

Actividad para la casa

Use 10 fichas, crayolas u otros objetos pequeños. Trabaje con su hijo para mostrar todas las maneras de formar 10. (1 + 9, 6 + 4 y así sucesivamente). Luego escriban juntos oraciones numéricas de suma para cada manera de formar diez.

Literatura

Busque este libro en una biblioteca. Pídale a su hijo que cuente cuántos objetos hay en cada página.

¿Cuántos caracoles?: Un libro para contar
por Paul Giganti.
Greenwillow Books, 1994

Algebra • Use Pictures to Add To

 COMMON CORE STANDARD—1.OA.1
Represent and solve problems involving addition and subtraction.

Write how many.

1.

5 horses   and   3 more horses   _____ horses

2.

3 dogs   and   2 more dogs   _____ dogs

3.

4 cats   and   1 more cat   _____ cats

Problem Solving Real World

There are 2 rabbits. 5 rabbits join them. How many rabbits are there now?

There are _____ rabbits.

Lesson Check (1.OA.1)

1. How many birds are there?

Write the number.

2 birds   and   6 more birds   ____ birds

Spiral Review (1.OA.1)

2. How many goats are there?

Write the number.

2 goats   and   4 more goats   ____ goats

3. How many rabbits are there?

Write the number.

5 rabbits   and   1 more rabbit   ____ rabbits

4. How many ducks are there?

Write the number.

5 ducks   and   4 more ducks   ____ ducks

Name _____

Model Adding To

Use ▢ to show adding to.
Draw the ▢. Write the sum.

COMMON CORE STANDARD—1.OA.1
Represent and solve problems involving addition and subtraction.

1. 5 ants and 1 more ant

$$5 + 1 = \underline{\quad}$$

2. 3 cats and 4 more cats

$$3 + 4 = \underline{\quad}$$

3. 4 dogs and 4 more dogs

$$4 + 4 = \underline{\quad}$$

4. 4 bees and 5 more bees

$$4 + 5 = \underline{\quad}$$

Problem Solving Real World

Use the picture to help you complete the
addition sentences. Write each sum.

5. ___ ■ + ___ ■ = ___ ■ in all

6. ___ ● + ___ ● = ___ ● in all

Lesson Check (1.OA.1)

1. Draw the 🔲. Write the sum. What is the sum of 4 and 2?

$$4 + 2 = \underline{}$$

Spiral Review (1.OA.1)

2. How many butterflies are there?
   Write the number.
   5 butterflies   and   2 more butterflies   _____ butterflies

3. Draw the 🔲. Write the sum. What is the sum of 2 and 3?

$$2 + 3 = \underline{}$$

4. How many birds are there?
   Write the number.
   6 birds   and   1 more bird   _____ birds

Model Putting Together

Use ⃝ to solve. Draw to show your work. Write the number sentence and how many.

COMMON CORE STANDARD—1.OA.1
Represent and solve problems involving addition and subtraction.

1. There are 2 big dogs and 4 small dogs. How many dogs are there?

   _____ dogs

   ___ ⃝ ___ ⃝ ___

2. There are 3 red crayons and 2 green crayons. How many crayons are there?

   _____ crayons

   ___ ⃝ ___ ⃝ ___

3. There are 5 brown rocks and 3 white rocks. How many rocks are there?

   _____ rocks

   ___ ⃝ ___ ⃝ ___

Problem Solving

4. Write your own addition story problem.

   _____
   - - - - - - - - - - - - - - - -
   _____
   - - - - - - - - - - - - - - - -
   _____

Lesson Check (1.OA.1)

1. Write the number sentence and how many. There are 3 black cats and 2 brown cats. How many cats are there?

   ____ cats   ____ ◯ ____ ◯ ____

....

2. There are 4 red flowers and 3 yellow flowers. How many flowers are there?

   ____ flowers

....

Spiral Review (1.OA.1)

3. How many turtles are there?
   Write the number.

   6 turtles   and   3 more turtles   ____ turtles

....

4. Draw the ⬚. Write the sum. What is the sum of 2 and 1?

   2 + 1 = ____

Problem Solving • Model Addition

COMMON CORE STANDARD—1.OA.1
Represent and solve problems involving addition and subtraction.

Read the problem. Use the bar model to solve. Complete the model and the number sentence.

1. Dylan has 7 flowers.
   4 of the flowers are red.
   The rest are yellow.
   How many flowers are yellow?

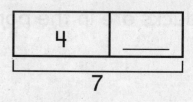

$$4 + \underline{} = 7$$

2. Some birds are flying in a group.
   4 more birds join the group.
   Then there are 9 birds in the group. How many birds were in the group before?

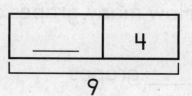

$$\underline{} + 4 = 9$$

3. 6 cats are walking.
   1 more cat walks with them.
   How many cats are walking now?

$$6 + 1 = \underline{}$$

Lesson Check (1.OA.1)

1. Complete the model and the number sentence. 3 ducks are in the pond. 6 more ducks join them. How many ducks are in the pond now?

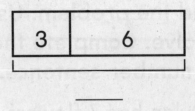

$3 + 6 = \underline{}$

Spiral Review (1.OA.1)

2. Write the number sentence and how many. There are 4 green grapes and 4 red grapes. How many grapes are there?

$\underline{}$ grapes

3. Draw the ☐. Write the sum. What is the sum of 7 and 3?

$7 + 3 = \underline{}$

4. Draw the ☐. Write the sum. What is the sum of 6 and 2?

$6 + 2 = \underline{}$

Algebra • Add Zero

**Draw circles to show the number.
Write the sum.**

COMMON CORE STANDARD—1.OA.3
Understand and apply properties of operations and the relationship between addition and subtraction.

1.

$3 + 0 =$ ___

2.

$0 + 5 =$ ___

3.

$1 + 3 =$ ___

4.

$5 + 1 =$ ___

Problem Solving Real World

Write the addition sentence to solve.

5. 6 turtles swim.
No turtles join them.
How many turtles are there now?   ___ + ___ = ___

___ turtles

Lesson Check (1.OA.3)

1. Draw ◯ to show each addend. Write the sum. What is the sum for 0 + 4?

$$0 + 4 = \underline{\quad}$$

Spiral Review (1.OA.1)

2. Complete the model and the number sentence. There are 4 goats in the barn. 3 more goats join them. How many goats are in the barn now?

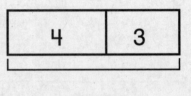

$$4 + 3 = \underline{\quad}$$

3. Write the number sentence and how many. There are 7 blue crayons and 1 yellow crayon. How many crayons are there?

____ crayons

4. Draw the ⬚. Write the sum. What is the sum of 3 and 3?

$$3 + 3 = \underline{\quad}$$

Name _____

Algebra • Add in Any Order

COMMON CORE STANDARD—1.OA.3
Understand and apply properties of operations and the relationship between addition and subtraction.

Use 🎲 🎲. Write the sum.
Circle the addition sentences
in each row that have the same
addends in a different order.

1. $1 + 3 =$ ___ $1 + 2 =$ ___ $3 + 1 =$ ___

2. $2 + 3 =$ ___ $3 + 2 =$ ___ $0 + 5 =$ ___

3. $2 + 4 =$ ___ $3 + 3 =$ ___ $4 + 2 =$ ___

4. $4 + 1 =$ ___ $1 + 4 =$ ___ $0 + 4 =$ ___

5. $3 + 6 =$ ___ $4 + 5 =$ ___ $5 + 4 =$ ___

Problem Solving

Draw pictures to match the addition sentences.
Write the sums.

6. $5 + 2 =$ ___

$2 + 5 =$ ___

Lesson Check (1.OA.3)

1. Circle the addition sentences in the row that have the same addends in a different order.

$$1 + 5 = 6 \qquad 6 + 1 = 7 \qquad 1 + 6 = 7$$

Spiral Review (1.OA.1, 1.OA.3)

2. Draw ◯ to show the numbers. Write the sum. What is the sum?

$$0 + 2 = \underline{\quad}$$

3. Write the number sentence and how many. There are 5 long strings and 3 short strings. How many strings are there?

_____ strings

4. Draw the ▢. Write the sum. What is the sum of 6 and 2?

$$6 + 2 = \underline{\quad}$$

Algebra • Put Together Numbers to 10

Use  . Color to show how to make 8. Complete the addition sentences.

COMMON CORE STANDARD—1.OA.1
Represent and solve problems involving addition and subtraction.

1. $8 = \underline{8} + \underline{0}$

2. $8 = \underline{} + \underline{}$

3. $8 = \underline{} + \underline{}$

4. $8 = \underline{} + \underline{}$

5. $8 = \underline{} + \underline{}$

6. $8 = \underline{} + \underline{}$

7. $8 = \underline{} + \underline{}$

8. $8 = \underline{} + \underline{}$

9. $8 = \underline{} + \underline{}$

Lesson Check (1.OA.1)

1. Show three different ways to make 10.

    $10 = \underline{\quad} + \underline{\quad}$ $10 = \underline{\quad} + \underline{\quad}$ $10 = \underline{\quad} + \underline{\quad}$

2. Show three different ways to make 6.

    $6 = \underline{\quad} + \underline{\quad}$ $6 = \underline{\quad} + \underline{\quad}$ $6 = \underline{\quad} + \underline{\quad}$

Spiral Review (1.OA.1, 1.OA.3)

3. Circle the number sentences that show the same addends in a different order.

    $4 + 2 = 6$ $1 + 5 = 6$ $2 + 4 = 6$

4. What is the sum for $2 + 0$? Write the sum.

    $2 + 0 = \underline{\quad}$

5. Complete the model and the number sentence. 3 rabbits sit in the grass. 4 more rabbits join them. How many rabbits are there now?

3	4

    ____ rabbits $3 + 4 = \underline{\quad}$

Addition to 10

COMMON CORE STANDARD—1.OA.6
Add and subtract within 20.

Write the sum.

1. $\begin{array}{r} 4 \\ +1 \\ \hline \end{array}$

2. $\begin{array}{r} 2 \\ +6 \\ \hline \end{array}$

3. $\begin{array}{r} 3 \\ +4 \\ \hline \end{array}$

4. $\begin{array}{r} 5 \\ +1 \\ \hline \end{array}$

5. $\begin{array}{r} 8 \\ +0 \\ \hline \end{array}$

6. $\begin{array}{r} 2 \\ +3 \\ \hline \end{array}$

7. $\begin{array}{r} 0 \\ +0 \\ \hline \end{array}$

8. $\begin{array}{r} 5 \\ +2 \\ \hline \end{array}$

9. $\begin{array}{r} 5 \\ +5 \\ \hline \end{array}$

10. $\begin{array}{r} 0 \\ +6 \\ \hline \end{array}$

11. $\begin{array}{r} 3 \\ +1 \\ \hline \end{array}$

12. $\begin{array}{r} 2 \\ +4 \\ \hline \end{array}$

Problem Solving Real World

Add. Write the sum. Use the sum and the key to color the flower.

13.

$4 + 5 = \underline{}$

KEY
6 YELLOW
7 RED
8 PURPLE
9 PINK

Lesson Check (1.OA.6)

I. Write the sum.

$$5 + 3$$

Spiral Review (1.OA.1)

2. Show three different ways to make 9.

$9 = \underline{\quad} + \underline{\quad}$ $9 = \underline{\quad} + \underline{\quad}$ $9 = \underline{\quad} + \underline{\quad}$

3. Complete the number sentence. There are
8 large stones and 2 small stones. How many
stones are there?

____ stones $8 + 2 = \underline{\quad}$

4. Complete the number sentence.
What is the sum of 2 and 2?

$2 + 2 = \underline{\quad}$

School-Home Letter

Dear Family,

My class started Chapter 2 this week. In this chapter, I will learn different ways to subtract. I will learn to write subtraction sentences.

Love, _____

Vocabulary

minus (−) part of a subtraction sentence that means "to take from"

$$minus$$
$$6 - 5 = 1$$

difference answer to a subtraction sentence

$$3 - 2 = \textcircled{1}$$

fewer smaller number of something 3 books and 2 bags, you have 1 fewer bag than books

Home Activity

Show your child two groups of household objects, such as spoons and forks. Have your child use subtraction to compare how many more or fewer. Use different amounts and different objects every day.

$$5 - 2 = ?$$

Literature

Look for these books in a library. Have your child compare groups of items using *more* and *fewer*.

More, Fewer, Less by Tana Hoban. Greenwillow Books, 1998.

Elevator Magic by Stuart J. Murphy. HarperCollins, 1997.

Carta para la casa

Querida familia:

Mi clase comenzó el Capítulo 2 esta semana. En este capítulo, aprenderé distintas formas para restar. Aprenderé a escribir enunciados de resta.

Con cariño, _____

Vocabulario

menos (−) parte de un enunciado de resta que significa "quitar de"

$$\text{menos}$$
$$6 - 5 = 1$$

diferencia respuesta a un enunciado de resta

$$3 - 2 = ①$$

menos un número Cantidad menor de algo. Si tienes 3 libros y 2 carteras, tienes 1 cartera menos.

Actividad para la casa

Muestre a su hijo dos grupos de objetos que haya en la casa, como cucharas y tenedores. Pídale que use la resta para comparar cuántos objetos más o menos hay de cada tipo. Use distintas cantidades y objetos diferentes cada día.

$$5 - 2 = ?$$

Literatura

Busque estos libros en una biblioteca. Pídale a su hijo que compare grupos de cosas usando *más* y *menos*.

More, Fewer, Less
por Tana Hoban. Greenwillow Books, 1998.

El ascensor maravilloso
por Stuart J. Murphy. HarperCollins, 1997.

Use Pictures to Show Taking From

Use the picture. Circle the part
you take from the whole group.
Then cross it out. Write how many
there are now.

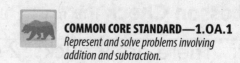

COMMON CORE STANDARD—1.OA.1
*Represent and solve problems involving
addition and subtraction.*

1.

3 cats   I cat walks away.   _____ cats now

2.

5 horses   2 horses walk away.   _____ horses now

3.

7 dogs   3 dogs walk away.   _____ dogs now

Problem Solving Real World

Solve.

4. There are 7 birds. 2 birds fly away.
   How many birds are there now?

   _____ birds

Lesson Check (1.OA.1)

1. There are 4 ducks. 2 ducks swim away.
   How many ducks are there now?

   ____ ducks

Spiral Review (1.OA.1, 1.OA.3, 1.OA.6)

2. What is the sum for $2 + 0$?

   Draw $\bigcirc$ to show each addend. Write the sum.

   $$2 + 0 = \underline{\quad}$$

3. How many birds? Write how many.

   5 birds   and   2 birds   ____ birds

4. What is the sum? Write the sum.

   $$\begin{array}{r} 6 \\ + 2 \\ \hline \end{array}$$

Model Taking From

COMMON CORE STANDARD—1.OA.1
Represent and solve problems involving addition and subtraction.

Use 🎲 to show taking from.
Draw the 🎲. Circle the part
you take from the group. Then
cross it out. Write the difference.

1. 4 turtles 1 turtle walks away.

$$4 - 1 = \underline{}$$

2. 8 birds 7 birds fly away.

$$8 - 7 = \underline{}$$

3. 6 bees 2 bees fly away.

$$6 - 2 = \underline{}$$

4. 7 swans 5 swans swim away.

$$7 - 5 = \underline{}$$

Problem Solving *Real World*

Draw 🎲 to solve. Complete
the subtraction sentence.

5. There are 8 fish.
4 fish swim away.
How many fish
are there now?

$$\underline{} - \underline{} = \underline{}$$

_____ fish

Lesson Check (1.OA.1)

1. Show taking from. Circle the part you take from the group. Then cross it out. Write the difference.

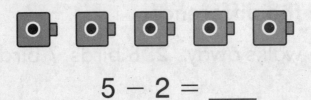

$$5 - 2 = \underline{\quad}$$

Spiral Review (1.OA.1, 1.OA.3)

2. How many snails? Write the number.

7 snails   and   I snail   _____ snails

3. Circle the number sentences that show the same addends in a different order.

$$7 + 1 = 8 \qquad 6 + 2 = 8 \qquad 2 + 6 = 8$$

Model Taking Apart

 COMMON CORE STANDARD—1.OA.1
Represent and solve problems involving addition and subtraction.

Use ● to solve. Draw to show your work. Write the number sentence and how many.

1. There are 7 bags. 2 bags are big. The rest are small. How many bags are small?

____ small bags   ____ ◯ ____ ◯ ____

2. There are 6 dogs. 4 dogs are brown. The rest are black. How many dogs are black?

___ ◯ ___ ◯ ___

____ black dogs

 Problem Solving *Real World*

Solve. Draw a model to explain.

3. There are 8 cats. 6 cats are white. The rest are black. How many cats are black?

____ black cats

Lesson Check (1.OA.1)

1. Solve. Draw a model to explain.
    There are 8 blocks. 3 blocks
    are white. The rest are blue.
    How many blocks are blue?

    _____ blue blocks

Spiral Review (1.OA.1)

2. Draw ◯ to solve. Write the number sentence
    and how many. There are 4 green grapes and
    5 red grapes. How many grapes are there?

    _____ grapes

3. Solve. Complete the model and the number
    sentence. 3 ducks swim in the pond. 2 more
    join them. How many ducks are in the pond
    now?

    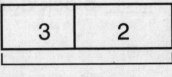

    3 + 2 = _____ ducks

4. Draw the 🎲 . Write the sum.
    What is the sum of 1 and 4?

    1 + 4 = _____

Problem Solving • Model Subtraction

COMMON CORE STANDARD—1.OA.1
Represent and solve problems involving addition and subtraction.

Read the problem. Use the model to solve. Complete the model and the number sentence.

1. There were 7 ducks in the pond. Some ducks swam away. Then there were 4 ducks. How many ducks swam away?

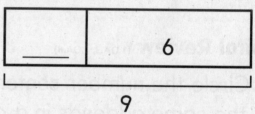

$$7 \ - \ \_\_\_ \ = \ 4$$

2. Tom had 9 gifts. He gave some away. Then there were 6 gifts. How many gifts did he give away?

$$9 \ - \ \_\_\_ \ = \ 6$$

3. Some ponies were in a barn. 3 ponies walked out. Then there were 2 ponies. How many ponies were in the barn before?

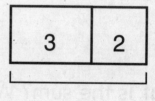

$$\_\_\_ \ - \ 3 \ = \ 2$$

4. There are 10 puppies. 3 puppies are brown. The rest are black. How many puppies are black?

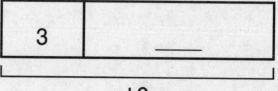

$$10 \ - \ 3 \ = \ \_\_\_$$

Lesson Check (1.OA.1)

1. Complete the model and the number sentence. There are 8 shells. 6 shells are white. The rest are pink. How many shells are pink?

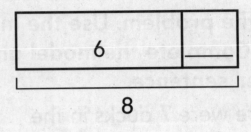

$$\underline{} \, 8 \, - \, \underline{} \, 6 \, = \, \underline{}$$

Spiral Review (1.OA.3, 1.OA.6)

2. Circle the number sentences that show the same addends in a different order.

$$6 - 2 = 4 \qquad 2 + 4 = 6 \qquad 4 + 2 = 6$$

3. What is the sum? Write the sum.

$$\begin{array}{r} 4 \\ + \, 3 \\ \hline \end{array}$$

Use Pictures and Subtraction to Compare

COMMON CORE STANDARD—1.OA.8
Work with addition and subtraction equations.

Draw lines to match.
Subtract to compare.

1.

$8 - 5 =$ _____

_____ more

2.

$9 - 4 =$ _____

_____ fewer

Problem Solving Real World

Draw a picture to show the problem.
Write a subtraction sentence to
match your picture.

3. Jo has 4 golf clubs and
2 golf balls. How many fewer
golf balls does Jo have?

_____ − _____ = _____

_____ fewer

Lesson Check (1.OA.8)

1. Draw lines to match. Subtract to compare.

How many fewer  are there?

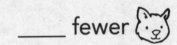

$4 - 3 =$ _____   _____ fewer 🐱

Spiral Review (1.OA.1, 1.OA.6)

2. Draw the ▢. Write the sum.
What is the sum of 5 and 1?

$5 + 1 =$ _____

3. Write the sum. What is the sum?

$$\begin{array}{r} 4 \\ + 5 \\ \hline \end{array}$$

4. How many flowers? Write the number.

4 flowers   and   3 flowers   _____ flowers

Subtract to Compare

COMMON CORE STANDARD—1.OA.1
Represent and solve problems involving addition and subtraction.

Read the problem. Use the bar model to solve. Write the number sentence. Then write how many.

1. Ben has 7 flowers. Tim has 5 flowers. How many fewer flowers does Tim have than Ben?

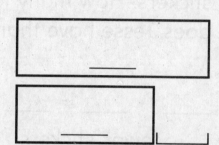

_____ fewer flowers

_____ ◯ _____ ◯ _____

2. Nicky has 8 toys. Ada has 3 toys. How many more toys does Nicky have than Ada?

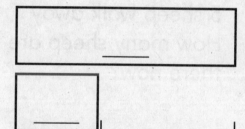

_____ more toys

_____ ◯ _____ ◯ _____

Problem Solving

Complete the number sentence to solve.

3. Maya has 7 pens. Sam has 1 pen. How many more pens does Maya have than Sam?

_____ − _____ = _____

_____ more pens

Lesson Check (1.OA.1)

1. Use the bar model to solve.
   Write the number sentence.
   Jesse has 2 stickers. Sara has 8
   stickers. How many fewer stickers
   does Jesse have than Sara?

   | 8 | |

   ___ − ___ = ___

   ___ fewer stickers

Spiral Review (1.OA.1)

2. Solve. There are 6 sheep.
   5 sheep walk away.
   How many sheep are
   there now?

   ___ sheep

3. Complete the bar model and
   the number sentence. 5 cows
   stand in a field. 2 more cows
   join them. How many cows are
   in the field now?

   | 5 | 2 |

   ___

   5 + 2 = ___

© Houghton Mifflin Harcourt Publishing Company

Subtract All or Zero

COMMON CORE STANDARD—1.OA.8
Work with addition and subtraction equations.

Complete the subtraction sentence.

1.

$$3 - 0 = \underline{\hphantom{00}}$$

2.

$$2 - 2 = \underline{\hphantom{00}}$$

3. $5 - 0 = \underline{\hphantom{00}}$

4. $\underline{\hphantom{00}} = 1 - 0$

5. $6 - 6 = \underline{\hphantom{00}}$

6. $0 = \underline{\hphantom{00}} - 8$

7. $7 - 0 = \underline{\hphantom{00}}$

8. $5 - \underline{\hphantom{00}} = 0$

Problem Solving

Write the number sentence
and tell how many.

9. There are 9 books on the shelf.
0 are blue and the rest are green.
How many books are green?

_____ green books

Lesson Check (1.OA.8)

I. Complete the subtraction sentence.
   What is the difference for 4 − 0?

   _____ − _____ = _____

2. Complete the subtraction sentence.
   What is the difference for 6 − 6?

   _____ − _____ = _____

Spiral Review (1.OA.1)

3. Write the number. How many bunnies?

   3 bunnies   and   3 bunnies   _____ bunnies

4. Complete an addition sentence for each model.

   _____ + _____ = 10

   _____ + _____ = 9

   _____ + _____ = 7

   _____ + _____ = 8

Algebra • Take Apart Numbers

COMMON CORE STANDARD—1.OA.1
Represent and solve problems involving addition and subtraction.

Use ⚅. Color and draw to show how to take apart 5. Complete the subtraction sentence.

1. ⬜⬜⬜⬜⬜   5 − ___ = ___

2. ⬜⬜⬜⬜⬜   5 − ___ = ___

3. ⬜⬜⬜⬜⬜   5 − ___ = ___

4. ⬜⬜⬜⬜⬜   5 − ___ = ___

5. ⬜⬜⬜⬜⬜   5 − ___ = ___

6. ⬜⬜⬜⬜⬜   5 − ___ = ___

Problem Solving

Solve.

7. Joe has 9 marbles. He gives them all to his sister. How many marbles does he have now?

___ marbles

Lesson Check (1.OA.1)

1. Draw the ⬚. Show a way to take apart 8. Complete a number sentence to match your model.

$$8 - \underline{\hspace{1cm}} = \underline{\hspace{1cm}}$$

Spiral Review (1.OA.1, 1.OA.6)

2. What is the sum? Write the sum.

$$\begin{array}{r} 6 \\ + 4 \\ \hline \end{array}$$

3. Solve. There are 7 fish. 3 fish swim away. How many fish are there now?

    _____ fish

4. Solve. There are 10 bugs. 8 hop away. How many bugs are there now?

    _____ bugs

Name _____

Subtraction from 10 or Less

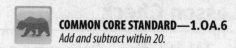

COMMON CORE STANDARD—1.OA.6
Add and subtract within 20.

Write the difference.

1. $\begin{array}{r} 5 \\ -1 \\ \hline \end{array}$

2. $\begin{array}{r} 3 \\ -2 \\ \hline \end{array}$

3. $\begin{array}{r} 8 \\ -3 \\ \hline \end{array}$

4. $\begin{array}{r} 6 \\ -4 \\ \hline \end{array}$

5. $\begin{array}{r} 7 \\ -0 \\ \hline \end{array}$

6. $\begin{array}{r} 5 \\ -3 \\ \hline \end{array}$

7. $\begin{array}{r} 4 \\ -4 \\ \hline \end{array}$

8. $\begin{array}{r} 8 \\ -1 \\ \hline \end{array}$

9. $\begin{array}{r} 8 \\ -7 \\ \hline \end{array}$

10. $\begin{array}{r} 6 \\ -3 \\ \hline \end{array}$

11. $\begin{array}{r} 5 \\ -5 \\ \hline \end{array}$

12. $\begin{array}{r} 7 \\ -6 \\ \hline \end{array}$

Problem Solving

Solve.

13. 6 birds are in the tree.
    None of the birds fly away.
    How many birds are left?

    _____ − _____ = _____

Lesson Check (1.OA.6)

I. Write the difference.

$$\begin{array}{r} 4 \\ -\ 0 \\ \hline \end{array}$$

Spiral Review (1.OA.1, 1.OA.3)

2. Solve. Write a number sentence.
There are 8 pens. 3 pens
are blue. The rest are red.
How many pens are red?

___ − ___ = ___

3. Circle the number sentences that show the same
addends in a different order.

$$4 + 5 = 9 \qquad 5 + 4 = 9 \qquad 9 - 4 = 5$$

School-Home Letter

Dear Family,

My class started Chapter 3 this week. In this chapter, I will learn about addition strategies such as counting on, adding doubles, and adding in any order.

Love, _____

Vocabulary

doubles Two equal groups make a doubles fact.

$2 + 2 = 4$

doubles plus one $2 + 2 = 4$, so $2 + 3$ is 1 more, or 5.

$2 + 3 = 5$

Home Activity

Have your child find objects that show doubles facts. For example, he or she may find a pair of shoes to show $1 + 1$, a carton of eggs to show $6 + 6$, or a six-pack of juice cans to show $3 + 3$. Ask your child to say those doubles facts.

Add another item to one of the groups, and have your child name the doubles plus one fact.

Literature

Look for these books in a library. Point out examples of doubles and counting on facts in the pictures.

12 Ways to Get to 11 by Eve Merriam. Aladdin, 1996.

Two of Everything: A Chinese Folktale by Lily Toy Hong. Albert Whitman and Company, 1993.

Carta para la casa

Querida familia:

Mi clase comenzó el Capítulo 3 esta semana. En este capítulo, aprenderé estrategias de suma como contar hacia adelante, sumar dobles y sumar en cualquier orden.

Con cariño, _____

Vocabulario

dobles Dos grupos iguales forman una operación de dobles.

$2 + 2 = 4$

dobles más uno $2 + 2 = 4$, por lo tanto $2 + 3$ es 1 más o 5.

$2 + 3 = 5$

Actividad para la casa

Pida a su hijo que encuentre objetos que muestren operaciones de dobles. Por ejemplo, puede hallar un par de zapatos para mostrar $1 + 1$, una caja de huevos para mostrar $6 + 6$ o una caja de 6 latas de jugo para mostrar $3 + 3$. Pídale a su hijo que le diga cuáles son las operaciones de dobles.

Agregue otro artículo a uno de los grupos y pida a su hijo que nombre la operación de dobles más uno.

Literatura

Busque estos libros en una biblioteca. Señale ejemplos de operaciones de dobles y de contar uno hacia delante en las imágenes.

12 Ways to Get to 11 por Eve Merriam. Aladdin, 1996.

Two of Everything: A Chinese Folktale por Lily Toy Hong. Albert Whitman and Company, 1993.

Name _____

Algebra • Add in Any Order

COMMON CORE STANDARD—1.OA.3
Understand and apply properties of operations and the relationship between addition and subtraction.

Add. Change the order of the addends. Add again.

1.
$$\begin{array}{r} 7 \\ + 3 \\ \hline \end{array} \qquad \begin{array}{r} \square \\ + \square \\ \hline \square \end{array}$$

2.
$$\begin{array}{r} 6 \\ + 3 \\ \hline \end{array} \qquad \begin{array}{r} \square \\ + \square \\ \hline \square \end{array}$$

3.
$$\begin{array}{r} 9 \\ + 8 \\ \hline \end{array} \qquad \begin{array}{r} \square \\ + \square \\ \hline \square \end{array}$$

4.
$$\begin{array}{r} 6 \\ + 5 \\ \hline \end{array} \qquad \begin{array}{r} \square \\ + \square \\ \hline \square \end{array}$$

5.
$$\begin{array}{r} 8 \\ + 1 \\ \hline \end{array} \qquad \begin{array}{r} \square \\ + \square \\ \hline \square \end{array}$$

6.
$$\begin{array}{r} 4 \\ + 7 \\ \hline \end{array} \qquad \begin{array}{r} \square \\ + \square \\ \hline \square \end{array}$$

Problem Solving Real World

Write two addition sentences you can use to solve the problem.

7. Camila has 5 pennies.
   Then she finds 4 more pennies.
   How many pennies does
   she have now?

   ___ + ___ = ___

   ___ + ___ = ___

Lesson Check (1.OA.3)

1. What is another way to write $7 + 6 = 13$?

   $6 + 7 = \underline{\quad}$

2. What is another way to write $6 + 8 = 14$?

   $8 + 6 = \underline{\quad}$

Spiral Review (1.OA.1, 1.OA.6)

3. What is the sum?
   Write the number.

   $$\begin{array}{r} 4 \\ + \ 3 \\ \hline \end{array}$$

4. How many nests are there?
   Write the number.

   2 nests   and   1 more nest   ___ nests

Name _____

Count On

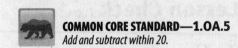

COMMON CORE STANDARD—1.OA.5
Add and subtract within 20.

Circle the greater addend.
Count on to find the sum.

1. $\begin{array}{r} 8 \\ + 2 \\ \hline \end{array}$ | 2. $\begin{array}{r} 1 \\ + 7 \\ \hline \end{array}$ | 3. $\begin{array}{r} 3 \\ + 9 \\ \hline \end{array}$ | 4. $\begin{array}{r} 5 \\ + 3 \\ \hline \end{array}$

5. $\begin{array}{r} 7 \\ + 3 \\ \hline \end{array}$ | 6. $\begin{array}{r} 3 \\ + 4 \\ \hline \end{array}$ | 7. $\begin{array}{r} 6 \\ + 2 \\ \hline \end{array}$ | 8. $\begin{array}{r} 1 \\ + 8 \\ \hline \end{array}$

Problem Solving

Draw to solve.
Write the addition sentence.

9. Jon eats 6 crackers.
   Then he eats 3 more crackers.
   How many crackers does he eat?

   ____ + ____ = ____ crackers

Lesson Check (1.OA.5)

1. Count on to solve $5 + 2$.
Write the sum.

____

2. Count on to solve $1 + 9$.
Write the sum.

____

Spiral Review (1.OA.1)

3. What does the model show?

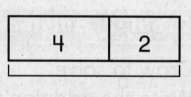

____ + ____ = ____

4. 4 ducks swim in the pond.
2 more ducks join them.
How many ducks are in
the pond now?

4	2

Complete the model and the number sentence.

$4 + 2 =$ ____

Add Doubles

 COMMON CORE STANDARD—1.OA.6
Add and subtract within 20.

Use 🎲. Draw 🎲 to show your work.
Write the sum.

1. $\begin{array}{r} 4 \\ +\ 4 \\ \hline \end{array}$

2. $\begin{array}{r} 6 \\ +\ 6 \\ \hline \end{array}$

3. $\begin{array}{r} 3 \\ +\ 3 \\ \hline \end{array}$

4. $\begin{array}{r} 8 \\ +\ 8 \\ \hline \end{array}$

5. $\begin{array}{r} 5 \\ +\ 5 \\ \hline \end{array}$

6. $\begin{array}{r} 7 \\ +\ 7 \\ \hline \end{array}$

Problem Solving

Write a doubles fact to solve.

7. There are 16 crayons in the box.
Some are green and some are red.
The number of green crayons is the
same as the number of red crayons.

_____ = _____ + _____

Lesson Check (1.OA.6)

1. Write a doubles fact with the sum of 18.

   ___ + ___ = 18

2. Write a doubles fact with the sum of 12.

   ___ + ___ = 12

Spiral Review (1.OA.1, 1.OA.3)

3. What is the sum of 3 and 2?
   Draw the ⬜. Write the sum.

   ___ + ___ = ___

4. Draw circles to show the numbers.
   Write the sum.

   4 + 0 = ___

Use Doubles to Add

COMMON CORE STANDARD—1.OA.6
Add and subtract within 20.

Use [dice]. Make doubles. Add.

1.

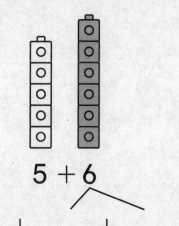

$5 + 6$

___ + ___ + ___

So, $5 + 6 =$ ___.

2.

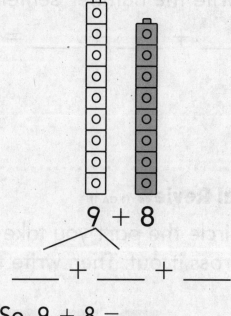

$9 + 8$

___ + ___ + ___

So, $9 + 8 =$ ___.

Use doubles to help you add.

3. $8 + 7 =$ ___

4. $6 + 5 =$ ___

5. $7 + 6 =$ ___

6. $4 + 5 =$ ___

7. $7 + 8 =$ ___

8. $8 + 9 =$ ___

Problem Solving

Solve. Draw or write to explain.

9. Bo has 6 toys. Mia has 7 toys.
How many toys do they have?

___ toys

Lesson Check (1.OA.6)

1. Use doubles to find the sum of $7 + 8$.

Write the number sentence.

___ + ___ + ___ = ___

Spiral Review (1.OA.1)

2. Circle the part you take from the group.
Cross it out. Then write the difference.

$$8 - 6 = \underline{\quad}$$

3. There are 7 gray kittens.
2 kittens are black. How many
fewer black kittens are there
than gray kittens?

Use the bar model to solve.

Then write the number sentence.

___ − ___ = ___

7

2

___

Name _____

Doubles Plus 1 and Doubles Minus 1

COMMON CORE STANDARD—1.OA.6
Add and subtract within 20.

Add. Write the doubles fact you used to solve the problem.

1. $7 + 8 =$ ___

___ ◯ ___ ◯ ___

2. $6 + 7 =$ ___

___ ◯ ___ ◯ ___

3. $4 + 3 =$ ___

___ ◯ ___ ◯ ___

4. $2 + 1 =$ ___

___ ◯ ___ ◯ ___

5. $8 + 9 =$ ___

___ ◯ ___ ◯ ___

6. $3 + 2 =$ ___

___ ◯ ___ ◯ ___

7. $5 + 6 =$ ___

___ ◯ ___ ◯ ___

8. $5 + 4 =$ ___

___ ◯ ___ ◯ ___

Problem Solving Real World

9. Andy writes an addition fact. One addend is 9. The sum is 17. What is the other addend? Write the addition fact.

___ + ___ = 17

I. Use the picture. Write a doubles plus one number sentence.

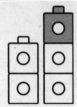

___ + ___ + ___

2. Which doubles fact helps you solve 8 + 7 = 15? Write the number sentence.

___ + ___ + ___

Spiral Review (1.OA.1)

3. There are 7 large dogs and 2 small dogs. How many dogs are there?

Use ◯ to solve. Draw to show your work. Write the number sentence and how many.

_____ dogs

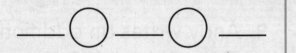

4. What is the sum of 2 and I more? Draw the ▣. Write the sum.

_____

2 + I = ___

Practice the Strategies

COMMON CORE STANDARD—1.OA.6
Add and subtract within 20.

Add. Color doubles facts (RED).
Color count on facts (BLUE).
Color doubles plus one or
doubles minus one facts (YELLOW).

1. $8 + 8 =$ _____

2. $8 + 1 =$ _____

3. $1 + 7 =$ _____

4. $8 + 3 =$ _____

5. $5 + 5 =$ _____

6. $8 + 7 =$ _____

7. $8 + 9 =$ _____

8. $6 + 3 =$ _____

9. $6 + 6 =$ _____

10. $2 + 5 =$ _____

11. $7 + 6 =$ _____

12. $5 + 4 =$ _____

Problem Solving Real World

Make a counting on problem.
Write the missing numbers.

13. _____ apples are in a bag.

_____ more apples are put in the bag.
How many apples are in the bag now?

_____ apples

Lesson Check (1.OA.6)

1. Which strategy would you use
to find $2 + 8$? Explain how you decided.

_____

_____

2. What is the sum of $9 + 9$?
Write the number.

_____

Spiral Review (1.OA.1, 1.OA.3)

3. What is the sum of $5 + 2$ or $2 + 5$?
Why is the sum the same?

_____

_____

4. How many flowers are there?
Write the number.

3 flowers   and   3 more flowers   _____ flowers

Name _____

Add 10 and More

 COMMON CORE STANDARD—1.OA.6
Add and subtract within 20.

Draw red ◯ to show 10. Draw
yellow ◯ to show the other addend.
Write the sum.

1.
$$\begin{array}{r} 10 \\ +\ \ 7 \\ \hline \end{array}$$

2.
$$\begin{array}{r} 10 \\ +\ \ 5 \\ \hline \end{array}$$

3.
$$\begin{array}{r} 10 \\ +\ \ 9 \\ \hline \end{array}$$

4.
$$\begin{array}{r} 10 \\ +\ \ 4 \\ \hline \end{array}$$

Problem Solving Real World

Draw red and yellow ◯ to solve.
Write the addition sentence.

5. Linda has 10 toy cars.
She gets 6 more cars.
How many toy cars
does she have now?

____ + ____ = ____ toy cars

Lesson Check (1.OA.6)

1. Draw more ⬤ to show the addition fact.
   Then solve.

   $\begin{array}{r} 10 \\ + \ 3 \\ \hline \end{array}$

   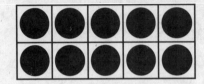 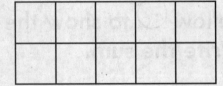

2. What number sentence does this model show?
   Write the number sentence.

   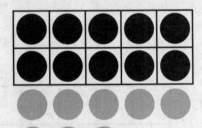

   ___ + ___ = ___

Spiral Review (1.OA.1)

3. Show three different ways to make 10.
   Write the number sentences.

   $10 = $ ___ $+$ ___ $10 = $ ___ $+$ ___ $10 = $ ___ $+$ ___

4. There are 3 large turtles and 1 small turtle.
   How many turtles are there?
   Write the number sentence and how many.

   ___ turtles

Name _____

Make a 10 to Add

COMMON CORE STANDARD—1.OA.6
Add and subtract within 20.

Use red and yellow ◯ and a ten frame.
Show both addends. Draw to make
a ten. Then write the new fact.
Add.

1. $\begin{array}{r} 5 \\ + 7 \\ \hline \end{array}$

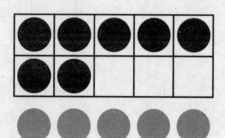

2. $\begin{array}{r} 9 \\ + 5 \\ \hline \end{array}$

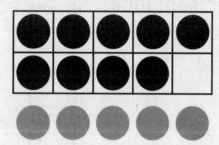

3. $\begin{array}{r} 8 \\ + 3 \\ \hline \end{array}$

Problem Solving *Real World*

Solve.

4. $10 + 6$ has the same sum as $7 +$ ____.

Lesson Check (1.OA.6)

1. What sum does this model show?
Write the number.

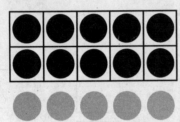   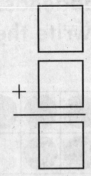

2. What addition sentence does this
model show? Write the number sentence.

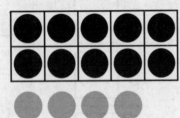   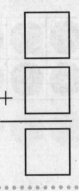

Spiral Review (1.OA.1, 1.OA.6)

3. What is the sum of $4 + 6$? Write the sum.

_____

4. There are 2 big flowers and 4 small flowers.
How many flowers are there?
Write the number sentence and how many.

_____ flowers

Name _____

Use Make a 10 to Add

COMMON CORE STANDARD—1.OA.6
Add and subtract within 20.

**Write to show how you make a ten.
Then add.**

1. What is $9 + 7$?

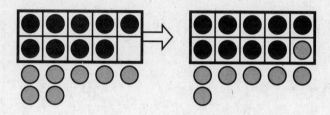

___ + ___ + ___

___ + ___ = ___

So, $9 + 7 =$ ___.

2. What is $5 + 8$?

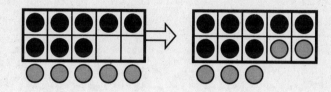

___ + ___ + ___

___ + ___ = ___

So, $5 + 8 =$ ___.

Problem Solving Real World

Use the clues to solve.
Draw lines to match.

3. Ann and Gia are eating grapes.
Ann eats 10 green grapes and
6 red grapes. Gia eats the same
number of grapes as Ann. Match
each person to her grapes.

Ann		7 green grapes and 9 red grapes
Gia		10 green grapes and 6 red grapes

Lesson Check (1.OA.6)

1. Write the number sentence.
   Make a ten to find $8 + 4$.
   Write the number sentence.

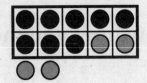

   ___ + ___ + ___ = ___

Spiral Review (1.OA.6, 1.OA.8)

2. What is the difference?
   Complete the subtraction sentence.

$$\begin{array}{r} 5 \\ -\,5 \\ \hline \end{array}$$

3. What is the difference?
   Write the difference.

$$\begin{array}{r} 8 \\ -\,2 \\ \hline \end{array}$$

Algebra • Add 3 Numbers

COMMON CORE STANDARD—1.OA.3
Understand and apply properties of operations and the relationship between addition and subtraction.

Look at the 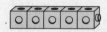 . Complete the addition sentences showing two ways to find the sum.

1. $5 + 4 + 2 = $ ___

___ + ___ = ___   ___ + ___ = ___

2. $2 + 2 + 6 = $ ___

___ + ___ = ___   ___ + ___ = ___

Problem Solving Real World

3. Choose three numbers from 1 to 6.
   Write the numbers in an addition sentence.
   Show two ways to find the sum.

Lesson Check (1.OA.3)

1. What is the sum of $3 + 4 + 2$?
Write the sum.

____

2. What is the sum of $5 + 1 + 4$?
Write the sum.

____

Spiral Review (1.OA.1, 1.OA.6)

3. What is the sum of 3 and 7?

$$\begin{array}{r} 3 \\ +\ 7 \\ \hline \end{array}$$

4. 4 cows are in the barn. 2 more cows join them. How many cows are in the barn now?

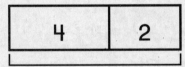

Complete the model and the number sentence.

____ cows $4 + 2 =$ ____

Name _____

Algebra • Add 3 Numbers

COMMON CORE STANDARD—1.OA.3
Understand and apply properties of operations and the relationship between addition and subtraction.

Choose a strategy.
Circle two addends to add first.
Write the sum.

1.
$$\begin{array}{r} 7 \\ 3 \\ +\ 3 \\ \hline \end{array}$$

2.
$$\begin{array}{r} 2 \\ 2 \\ +\ 6 \\ \hline \end{array}$$

3.
$$\begin{array}{r} 6 \\ 6 \\ +\ 3 \\ \hline \end{array}$$

4.
$$\begin{array}{r} 2 \\ 0 \\ +\ 8 \\ \hline \end{array}$$

5.
$$\begin{array}{r} 1 \\ 2 \\ +\ 9 \\ \hline \end{array}$$

6.
$$\begin{array}{r} 6 \\ 4 \\ +\ 3 \\ \hline \end{array}$$

7.
$$\begin{array}{r} 3 \\ 3 \\ +\ 5 \\ \hline \end{array}$$

8.
$$\begin{array}{r} 4 \\ 4 \\ +\ 8 \\ \hline \end{array}$$

Problem Solving

Draw a picture. Write the number sentence.

9. Don has 4 black dogs.
   Tim has 3 small dogs.
   Sue has 3 big dogs.
   How many dogs do they have?

   ___ + ___ + ___ = ___ dogs

I. What is the sum of $4 + 4 + 2$?

____

2. Circle two addends to add first.
   Find the sum. Explain your strategy.

$$\begin{array}{r} 7 \\ 3 \\ + 2 \\ \hline \end{array}$$

_____

_____

Spiral Review (1.OA.6)

3. Write a doubles plus one fact for the sum of 7.

____ + ____ = ____

4. What addition sentence does this model show?
   Write the number sentence.

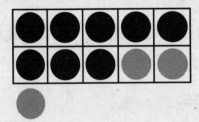

____ + ____ = ____

Problem Solving • Use Addition Strategies

COMMON CORE STANDARD—1.OA.2
Represent and solve problems involving addition and subtraction.

Draw a picture to solve.

1. Franco has 5 crayons. He gets 8 more crayons. Then he gets 2 more crayons. How many crayons does he have now?

___ ◯ ___ ◯ ___ ◯ ___

_____ crayons

2. Jackson has 6 blocks. He gets 5 more blocks. Then he gets 3 more blocks. How many blocks does he have now?

___ ◯ ___ ◯ ___ ◯ ___

_____ blocks

3. Avni has 7 gifts. Then he gets 2 more gifts. Then he gets 3 more gifts. How many gifts does Avni have now?

___ ◯ ___ ◯ ___ ◯ ___

_____ gifts

4. Meeka has 4 rings. She gets 2 more rings. Then she gets 1 more ring. How many rings does she have now?

___ ◯ ___ ◯ ___ ◯ ___

_____ rings

Lesson Check (1.OA.2)

1. Lila has 3 gray stones.
   She has 4 black stones.
   She also has 7 white stones.
   How many stones does she have?
   Write the number sentence.

   _____ stones

2. Patrick has 3 red stickers, 6 pink
   stickers, and 8 green stickers. How
   many stickers does Patrick have?
   Write the number sentence.

   _____ stickers

Spiral Review (1.OA.1, 1.OA.3)

3. What is the sum of 2 + 4 or 4 + 2?
   Write the number.

   _____

4. There are 6 black pens.
   There are 3 blue pens.
   How many pens are there?
   Write the number.

   _____ pens

School-Home Letter

Dear Family,

My class started Chapter 4 this week. In this chapter, I will learn about subtraction strategies and how to solve subtraction word problems.

Love, _____

Vocabulary

count back a way to subtract by counting back from the larger number

$$8 - 1 = 7$$

Start at 8.
Count back 1.
You are on 7.

Home Activity

Have your child practice counting from 1 to 8 and then from 8 to 1. Display numbers 1–8 on a piece of poster board or notebook paper. Each day, work with your child to solve simple subtraction problems by counting back 1, 2, or 3 using the list of numbers.

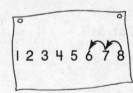

$$8 - 2 = 6$$

Literature

Look for these books in a library. Reading them together will reinforce your child's learning.

Monster Musical Chairs by Stuart J. Murphy. HarperCollins Children's Books, 2000.

Ten Little Ladybugs by Melanie Gerth. Piggy Toes Press, 2001.

Carta para la casa

Querida familia:

Mi clase comenzó hoy el Capítulo 4. En este capítulo, aprenderé estrategias de resta y a resolver problemas de resta en palabras.

Con cariño, _____

Vocabulario

contar hacia atrás un modo de restar contando hacia atrás de un número mayor

$$8 - 1 = 7$$

Comienza en 8.
Cuenta hacia atrás 1.
Quedas en 7.

Actividad para la casa

Pida a su hijo que cuente de 1 a 8 y de 8 a 1. Muestre los números de 1 a 8 en una cartulina o una hoja de cuaderno. Cada día, practique con su hijo resolver problemas simples de resta contando hacia atrás 1, 2 ó 3, en la lista de los números anotados.

$$8 - 2 = 6$$

Literatura

Busquen estos libros en la biblioteca. Si los lee con su hijo, ayudará a reforzar su aprendizaje.

Monster Musical Chairs
Stuart J. Murphy. HarperCollins Children's Books, 2000.

Ten Little Ladybugs
Melanie Gerth. Piggy Toes Press, 2001.

Count Back

COMMON CORE STANDARD—1.OA.5
Add and subtract within 20.

Count back 1, 2, or 3. Write the difference.

1. ___ $= 7 - 3$

2. $8 - 3 =$ ___

3. $4 - 3 =$ ___

4. ___ $= 9 - 1$

5. ___ $= 7 - 1$

6. ___ $= 6 - 2$

7. $6 - 1 =$ ___

8. $5 - 3 =$ ___

9. ___ $= 11 - 3$

10. $5 - 2 =$ ___

11. $10 - 2 =$ ___

12. ___ $= 10 - 3$

13. ___ $= 9 - 3$

14. $4 - 2 =$ ___

15. ___ $= 7 - 2$

16. ___ $= 12 - 3$

17. $8 - 1 =$ ___

18. $11 - 2 =$ ___

19. ___ $= 9 - 2$

20. $3 - 1 =$ ___

21. ___ $= 4 - 1$

Problem Solving

Write a subtraction sentence to solve.

22. Tina has 12 pencils.
    She gives away 3 pencils.
    How many pencils are left?

___ − ___ = ___

___ pencils

Lesson Check (1.OA.5)

1. Count back 3. What is the difference?
   Write the number.

   $$\_\_\_ = 10 - 3$$

2. Count back 2. What is the difference?
   Write the number.

   $$7 - 2 = \_\_\_$$

Spiral Review (1.OA.1, 1.OA.6)

3. Write a doubles fact to solve.
   Kai has 14 marbles. Some are blue
   and some are yellow. The number
   of blue marbles is the same as the
   number of yellow marbles.

   $$\_\_\_ = \_\_\_ + \_\_\_$$

4. Draw a picture to find the sum.
   Write the number sentence.
   There are 4 big dogs and
   3 small dogs. How many
   dogs are there?

   $$\_\_\_ + \_\_\_ = \_\_\_$$

Name _____

Think Addition to Subtract

 COMMON CORE STANDARD—1.OA.4
Understand and apply properties of operations and the relationship between addition and subtraction.

Use ⬜⬜ **to add and to subtract.**

1.
$$\begin{array}{r} 9 \\ -\ 3 \\ \hline ? \end{array}$$

Think
$$\begin{array}{r} 3 \\ +\ \square \\ \hline 9 \end{array}$$

So
$$\begin{array}{r} 9 \\ -\ 3 \\ \hline \end{array}$$

2.
$$\begin{array}{r} 15 \\ -\ 8 \\ \hline ? \end{array}$$

Think
$$\begin{array}{r} 8 \\ +\ \square \\ \hline 15 \end{array}$$

So
$$\begin{array}{r} 15 \\ -\ 8 \\ \hline \end{array}$$

3.
$$\begin{array}{r} 11 \\ -\ 7 \\ \hline ? \end{array}$$

Think
$$\begin{array}{r} 7 \\ +\ \square \\ \hline 11 \end{array}$$

So
$$\begin{array}{r} 11 \\ -\ 7 \\ \hline \end{array}$$

4.
$$\begin{array}{r} 13 \\ -\ 4 \\ \hline ? \end{array}$$

Think
$$\begin{array}{r} 4 \\ +\ \square \\ \hline 13 \end{array}$$

So
$$\begin{array}{r} 13 \\ -\ 4 \\ \hline \end{array}$$

5.
$$\begin{array}{r} 14 \\ -\ 6 \\ \hline ? \end{array}$$

Think
$$\begin{array}{r} 6 \\ +\ \square \\ \hline 14 \end{array}$$

So
$$\begin{array}{r} 14 \\ -\ 6 \\ \hline \end{array}$$

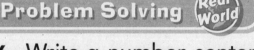 **Problem Solving**

6. Write a number sentence to solve.
   I have 18 pieces of fruit.
   9 are apples.
   The rest are oranges.
   How many are oranges?

____ oranges

Lesson Check (1.OA.4)

1. Use the sum of $7 + 9$ to solve $16 - 9$.

$7 + 9 =$ ___ $16 - 9 =$ ___

2. What is the missing number?

$$5 + \boxed{} = 14$$

$$14 - 5 = \boxed{}$$

Spiral Review (1.OA.1, 1.OA.3)

3. Use 🎲 🎲 🎲 to model the 3 addends.
Write the sum.

$4 + 4 + 6 =$ ___

4. Draw a picture to show your
work. Write the number.
There are 5 birds. 3 birds
fly away. How many birds
are there now?

____ birds

Use Think Addition to Subtract

COMMON CORE STANDARD—1.OA.4
Understand and apply properties of operations and the relationship between addition and subtraction.

Think of an addition fact to help you subtract.

1.
$$\begin{array}{r} 13 \\ -\ 8 \\ \hline \end{array}$$

$$\begin{array}{r} 8 \\ +\ \square \\ \hline 13 \end{array}$$

2.
$$\begin{array}{r} 12 \\ -\ 6 \\ \hline \end{array}$$

$$\begin{array}{r} 6 \\ +\ \square \\ \hline 12 \end{array}$$

3.
$$\begin{array}{r} 6 \\ -\ 4 \\ \hline \end{array}$$

4.
$$\begin{array}{r} 14 \\ -\ 9 \\ \hline \end{array}$$

5.
$$\begin{array}{r} 9 \\ -\ 5 \\ \hline \end{array}$$

6.
$$\begin{array}{r} 13 \\ -\ 6 \\ \hline \end{array}$$

7.
$$\begin{array}{r} 10 \\ -\ 7 \\ \hline \end{array}$$

8.
$$\begin{array}{r} 12 \\ -\ 4 \\ \hline \end{array}$$

9.
$$\begin{array}{r} 16 \\ -\ 7 \\ \hline \end{array}$$

10.
$$\begin{array}{r} 11 \\ -\ 8 \\ \hline \end{array}$$

11.
$$\begin{array}{r} 14 \\ -\ 8 \\ \hline \end{array}$$

12.
$$\begin{array}{r} 15 \\ -\ 7 \\ \hline \end{array}$$

Problem Solving

13. Solve. Draw or write to show your work.
I have 15 nickels.
Some are old. 6 are new.
How many nickels are old?

_____ nickels

Lesson Check (1.OA.4)

1. Use $9 + \underline{} = 13$ to find the difference.

$$9 + \underline{} = 13 \qquad\qquad 13 - 9 = \underline{}$$

2. Use $8 + \underline{} = 11$ to find the difference.

$$8 + \underline{} = 11 \qquad\qquad 11 - 8 = \underline{}$$

Spiral Review (1.OA.5, 1.OA.6)

3. Add. Write the doubles fact you used to solve the problem.

$$4 + 5 = \underline{}$$

$$\underline{} \bigcirc \underline{} \bigcirc \underline{}$$

4. Circle the greater addend.
   Count on to find the sum.

$$7 + 2 = \underline{}$$

Use 10 to Subtract

COMMON CORE STANDARD—1.OA.6
Add and subtract within 20.

Use ⬤ and ten frames. Make a ten to subtract.
Draw to show your work.

1.

$12 - 9 = \underline{\ ?\ }$

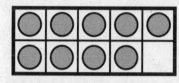

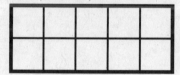

$12 - 9 = \underline{\qquad}$

2.

$12 - 8 = \underline{\ ?\ }$

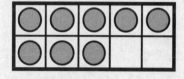

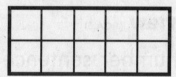

$12 - 8 = \underline{\qquad}$

Problem Solving Real World

Solve. Use the ten frames to make a ten to help you subtract.

3. Marta has 15 stickers.
8 are blue and the rest are red.
How many stickers are red?

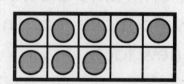

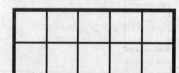

$\underline{\qquad}$ stickers

Lesson Check (1.OA.6)

1. Look at the model. Write the subtraction sentence that the model shows.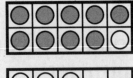

____ – ____ = ____

Spiral Review (1.OA.6)

2. What number sentence does this model show?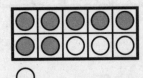

____ ◯ ____ ◯ ____

3. This ten frame shows 5 + 8. Draw to make ten. Then write the new fact.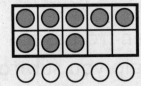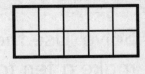

☐
+ ☐
———
☐

Name _____

Break Apart to Subtract

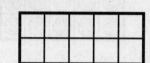
COMMON CORE STANDARD—1.OA.6
Add and subtract within 20.

Subtract.

I. What is 13 − 5?

Step 1	Step 2

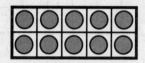 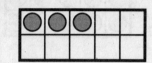   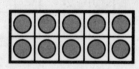 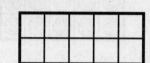

So, 13 − 5 = ____.

Problem Solving Real World

Use the ten frames. Write a number sentence.

2. There are 17 goats in the barn. 8 goats go outside. How many goats are still in the barn?

Step 1	Step 2

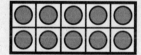 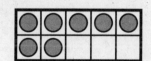   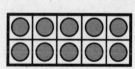 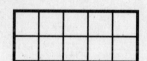

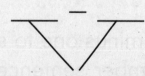

So, ____ − ____ = ____.

Lesson Check (1.OA.6)

1. Show how to make a ten to find $12 - 4$.
Write the number sentence.

Step 1

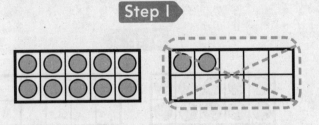

Step 2

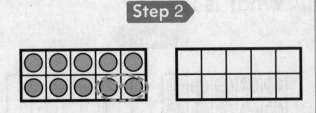

___ − ___ − ___ = ___

Spiral Review (1.OA.1, 1.OA.6)

2. Use ▢. Color and draw to show a way to take
apart 7. Complete the subtraction sentence.

$7 - \underline{} = \underline{}$

3. Use doubles minus one to solve $8 + 7$.
Write the number sentence.

___ ◯ ___ ◯ ___ ◯ ___

Problem Solving • Use Subtraction Strategies

COMMON CORE STANDARD—1.OA.1
Represent and solve problems involving addition and subtraction.

**Act it out to solve.
Draw to show your work.**

1. There are 13 monkeys. 6 are small. The rest are big. How many monkeys are big?

   $13 - 6 = \boxed{}$

   ____ monkeys are big.

2. Mindy had 13 flowers. She gave some to Sarah. She has 9 left. How many flowers did she give to Sarah?

   $13 - \boxed{} = 9$

   Mindy gave ____ flowers to Sarah.

3. There are 5 more horses in the barn than outside. 12 horses are in the barn. How many horses are outside?

   $12 - 5 = \boxed{}$

   ____ horses are outside.

4. Kim has 15 pennies. John has 6 pennies. How many fewer pennies does John have than Kim?

   $15 - 6 = \boxed{}$

   John has ____ fewer pennies.

Lesson Check (1.OA.1)

1. Solve. Complete the number sentence. Jack has 14 oranges. He gives some away. He has 6 left. How many oranges did he give away?

$$14 - \underline{} = 6$$

Jack gave away ___ oranges.

2. Solve. Complete the number sentence. 13 pears are in a basket. Some are yellow and some are green. 5 pears are green. How many pears are yellow?

$$13 - 5 = \underline{}$$

___ pears are yellow.

Spiral Review (1.OA.2, 1.OA.6)

3. Draw a picture to solve. Rita has 4 plants. She gets 9 more plants. Then Rita gets 1 more plant. How many plants does she have now?

___ ◯ ___ ◯ ___ ◯ ___

___ plants.

4. What is the sum of 10 + 5?

___

Chapter 5

School-Home Letter

Dear Family,

My class started Chapter 5 this week. In this chapter, I will learn how addition and subtraction are related. I will also learn how to identify and use related facts.

Love, _____

Vocabulary

related facts Related facts are facts that have the same parts and whole.

$$5 + 7 = 12$$
$$12 - 7 = 5$$

Home Activity

Make a poster with your child like the one below. Each day, write a different related fact. As you progress, leave spaces blank for your child to find missing numbers.

$$\_\_ + 3 = 5 \qquad 5 - 2 = 3$$
$$3 + \_\_ = 5 \qquad 5 - 3 = 2$$

Literature

Look for these books in a library. Read them together to reinforce learning.

Elevator Magic by Stuart J. Murphy. HarperCollins, 1997.

Animals on Board by Stuart J. Murphy. HarperCollins, 1998.

© Houghton Mifflin Harcourt Publishing Company

Chapter 5 · seventy-nine **P79**

Carta
para la casa

Querida familia:

Mi clase comenzó el Capítulo 5 esta semana. En este capítulo, aprenderé cómo se relacionan la suma y la resta. También aprenderé cómo identi car las operaciones relacionadas.

Con cariño, _____

Vocabulario

Operaciones relacionadas Las operaciones relacionadas son operaciones que usan los mismos números.

$$5 + 7 = 12$$
$$12 - 7 = 5$$

Actividad para la casa

Haga un cartel con su hijo como el que está abajo. Cada día, escriba una operación relacionada distinta. A medida que avanzan, deje espacios en blanco para que su hijo complete los números que faltan.

__ + 3 = 5	5 − 2 = 3
3 + __ = 5	5 − 3 = 2

Literatura

Busque estos libros en una biblioteca. Léanlos juntos para reforzar el aprendizaje.

Elevator Magic
por Stuart J. Murphy.
Harper Collins, 1997.

Animals on Board
Por Stuart J. Murphy.
Harper Collins, 1998.

Name _____

Add or Subtract

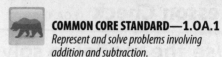

COMMON CORE STANDARD—1.OA.1
Represent and solve problems involving addition and subtraction.

Make a model to solve.

1. Stan has 12 pennies.

Some pennies are new.

4 pennies are old.

How many pennies are new?

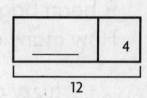

_____ new pennies

2. Liz has 9 toy bears.

Then she buys some more.

Now she has 15 toy bears.

How many toy bears did she buy?

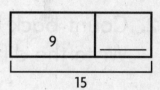

_____ toy bears

3. Eric buys 6 books.

Now he has 16 books.

How many books did he have to start?

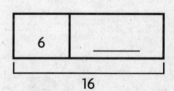

_____ books

4. Cho has 10 rings.

Some rings are silver.

4 rings are gold.

How many rings are silver?

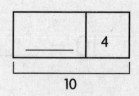

_____ silver rings

Lesson Check (1.OA.1)

Use the model to solve.

1. Arlo has 17 bean bag animals.
   Some are fuzzy.
   9 bean bag animals are not fuzzy.
   How many animals are fuzzy?

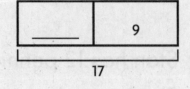

   _____ fuzzy animals

Spiral Review (1.OA.1, 1.OA.5)

2. Count back 1, 2, or 3.
   Write the difference.

$$\underline{} = 11 - 3$$

3. Use ⚀ ⚀. Color to show how to make ten.
   Complete the addition sentence.

○	○	○	○	○	○	○	○	○	○

   $10 = \underline{} + \underline{}$

Record Related Facts

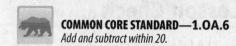

COMMON CORE STANDARD—1.OA.6
Add and subtract within 20.

Use 🎲🎲. Add or subtract. Complete the related facts.

1. $4 + \boxed{} = 12$ $\boxed{} - 8 = 4$

$8 + 4 = \boxed{}$ $\boxed{} - \boxed{} = \boxed{}$

2. $\boxed{} + 4 = 9$ $9 - 4 = \boxed{}$

$\boxed{} + 5 = 9$ $\boxed{} - \boxed{} = \boxed{}$

3. $9 + 7 = \boxed{}$ $16 - 7 = \boxed{}$

$7 + \boxed{} = 16$ $\boxed{} - \boxed{} = \boxed{}$

4. $\boxed{} + 6 = 14$ $14 - \boxed{} = 8$

$6 + 8 = \boxed{}$ $\boxed{} - \boxed{} = \boxed{}$

Problem Solving (Real World)

Choose a way to solve.
Write or draw to explain.

5. There are 16 apples on
the tree. No apples fall off.
How many apples are still on the tree?

_____ apples

Lesson Check (1.OA.6)

1. Write a related fact.

$$7 + 4 = 11 \qquad 11 - 7 = 4$$
$$4 + 7 = 11 \qquad \Box - \Box = \Box$$

. . . .

Spiral Review (1.OA.4, 1.OA.8)

2. Complete the subtraction sentence.

$$6 - 6 = \underline{\quad}$$

. . . .

3. Write an addition sentence that helps you solve $15 - 9$.

$$\underline{\quad} + \underline{\quad} = \underline{\quad}$$

Name _____

Identify Related Facts

COMMON CORE STANDARD—1.OA.6
Add and subtract within 20.

Add and subtract.
Circle the related facts.

1. $5 + 6 = $ ___

   $11 - 6 = $ ___

2. $4 + 9 = $ ___

   $9 - 4 = $ ___

3. $4 + 7 = $ ___

   $11 - 7 = $ ___

4. $9 + 8 = $ ___

   $17 - 8 = $ ___

5. $5 + 7 = $ ___

   $7 - 5 = $ ___

6. $6 + 8 = $ ___

   $14 - 8 = $ ___

7. $4 + 6 = $ ___

   $10 - 5 = $ ___

8. $9 + 5 = $ ___

   $14 - 5 = $ ___

Problem Solving Real World

9. Use the numbers to write related addition
   and subtraction sentences.

 6 7 8 9 15 16 17

   ___ $+$ ___ $=$ ___   ___ $-$ ___ $=$ ___

Lesson Check (1.OA.6)

1. Write a related fact for $7 + 6 = 13$.

___ ◯ ___ = ___

· ·

Spiral Review (1.OA.6, 1.OA.8)

2. Draw lines to match. Subtract to compare.
How many fewer 🪶 than 🐦 are there?

___ − ___ = ___   ___ fewer

· ·

3. Use doubles to help you add $7 + 8$.

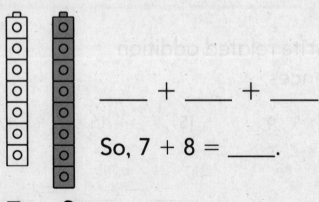

___ + ___ + ___

So, $7 + 8 = $ ___.

$7 + 8$

Use Addition to Check Subtraction

COMMON CORE STANDARD—1.OA.6
Add and subtract within 20.

Subtract. Then add to check your answer.

1. $12 - 4 = \boxed{}$

   $\boxed{} + 4 = \boxed{}$

2. $15 - 9 = \boxed{}$

   $\boxed{} + 9 = \boxed{}$

3. $17 - 8 = \boxed{}$

   $\boxed{} + 8 = \boxed{}$

4. $14 - 6 = \boxed{}$

   $\boxed{} + 6 = \boxed{}$

Problem Solving

Subtract.
Then add to check your answer.

5. There are 13 grapes in a bowl.
   Justin ate some of them.
   Now there are only 7 grapes left.
   How many grapes did Justin eat?

   ___ − ___ = ___   ___ grapes.

   ___ + ___ = ___

Lesson Check (1.OA.6)

1. Subtract. Then add to check your answer.

$$11 - 3 = \boxed{}$$

___ + ___ = ___

2. Subtract. Then add to check your answer.

$$12 - 8 = \boxed{}$$

___ + ___ = ___

Spiral Review (1.OA.1, 1.OA.3)

3. Jonas picks 10 peaches.
   4 peaches are small.
   The rest are big.
   How many are big?

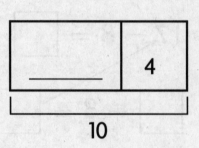

___ big peaches

4. Circle two addends to add first. Write the sum.

$$\begin{array}{r} 3 \\ 3 \\ +\,4 \\ \hline \end{array}$$

_____

Algebra • Unknown Numbers

COMMON CORE STANDARD—1.OA.8
Work with addition and subtraction equations.

Write the missing numbers.
Use 🎲 🎲 if you need to.

1. $6 + \boxed{} = 13$

   $13 - 6 = \boxed{}$

2. $9 + \boxed{} = 14$

   $14 - 9 = \boxed{}$

3. $\boxed{} + 7 = 15$

   $15 - 7 = \boxed{}$

4. $\boxed{} + 3 = 12$

   $12 - \boxed{} = 3$

5. $\boxed{} = 9 + 8$

   $8 = \boxed{} - 9$

6. $\boxed{} = 8 + 8$

   $8 = \boxed{} - 8$

Problem Solving Real World

Use cubes or draw a picture to solve.

7. Sally has 9 toy trucks.
   She gets 3 more toy trucks.
   How many toy trucks does
   she have now? _____ toy trucks

Lesson Check (1.OA.8)

1. Write the unknown number.

$$9 + \boxed{} = 16$$

Spiral Review (1.OA.3, 1.OA.6)

2. What is $14 - 6$?

Step 1

Step 2

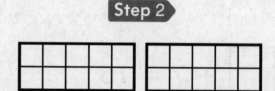

So, $14 - 6 =$ ___.

3. Draw circles to show the number.
Write the sum. $0 + 8$

$$0 + 8 = \underline{}$$

© Houghton Mifflin Harcourt Publishing Company

P90 ninety

Name _____

Algebra • Use Related Facts

COMMON CORE STANDARD—1.OA.8
Work with addition and subtraction equations.

Write the missing numbers.

1. Find $16 - 9$.

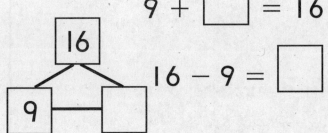

$9 + \boxed{} = 16$

$16 - 9 = \boxed{}$

2. Find $12 - 7$.

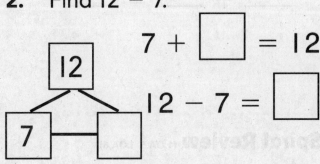

$7 + \boxed{} = 12$

$12 - 7 = \boxed{}$

3. Find $15 - 6$.

$6 + \boxed{} = 15$

$15 - 6 = \boxed{}$

4. Find $18 - 9$.

$9 + \boxed{} = 18$

$18 - 9 = \boxed{}$

Problem Solving Real World

Look at the shapes in the addition sentence.
Draw a shape to show a related subtraction fact.

5.

Lesson Check (1.OA.8)

1. Write an addition fact that helps you solve $12 - 4$.

   ___ + ___ = ___

Spiral Review (1.OA.5, 1.OA.6)

2. Circle the greater addend.
   Count on to find the sum.

$$\begin{array}{r} 9 \\ + 3 \\ \hline \end{array}$$

3. Draw ⚄ to show the doubles fact.
   Write the sum.

$$\begin{array}{r} 8 \\ + 8 \\ \hline \end{array}$$

Choose an Operation

COMMON CORE STANDARD—1.OA.1
Represent and solve problems involving addition and subtraction.

Circle add or subtract.
Write a number sentence to solve.

1. Adam has a bag of 11 pretzels. He eats 2 of the pretzels. How many pretzels are left?

   add   subtract

   _____

   _____ pretzels

2. Greta makes 3 drawings. Kate makes 4 more drawings than Greta. How many drawings does Kate make?

   add   subtract

   _____

   _____ drawings

Problem Solving *Real World*

Choose a way to solve.
Write or draw to explain.

3. Greg has 11 shirts.
   3 have long sleeves.
   The rest have short sleeves.
   How many short-sleeve shirts does Greg have?

   _____ short-sleeve shirts

Lesson Check (1.OA.1)

1. Circle add or subtract. Write a number sentence to solve. There are 18 children on the bus. Then 9 children get off. How many children are left on the bus?

add   subtract

___ ◯ ___ = ___

Spiral Review (1.OA.1, 1.OA.3)

2. Choose a way to solve. Draw or write to explain. Mike has 13 plants. He gives some away. He has 4 left. How many plants does he give away?

____ plants

3. Write the numbers 3, 2, and 8 in an addition sentence. Show two more ways to find the sum.

___ + ___ + ___ = ___

___ + ___ = ___

___ + ___ = ___

Algebra • Ways to Make Numbers to 20

COMMON CORE STANDARD—1.OA.6
Add and subtract within 20.

Use ⬛⬜⬛. Write ways to make the number at the top.

1. 10

$$2 + 7 + 1$$
$$5 + 5$$
$$10 - 0$$
$$9 \;⊕\; 1$$

2. 13

$$\_\_ + \_\_ + \_\_$$
$$\_\_ + \_\_$$
$$\_\_ - \_\_$$
$$\_\_ \;\bigcirc\; \_\_$$

3. 16

$$\_\_ + \_\_ + \_\_$$
$$\_\_ + \_\_$$
$$\_\_ - \_\_$$
$$\_\_ \;\bigcirc\; \_\_$$

4. 12

$$\_\_ + \_\_ + \_\_$$
$$\_\_ + \_\_$$
$$\_\_ - \_\_$$
$$\_\_ \;\bigcirc\; \_\_$$

Problem Solving Real World

Write numbers to make each line have the same sum.

5.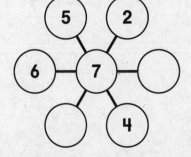

Lesson Check (1.OA.6)

1. Write ways to make 18.

18

___ + ___ + ___

___ + ___

___ − ___

___ ⊕ ___

2. Write ways to make 9.

9

___ + ___ + ___

___ + ___

___ − ___

___ ⊕ ___

Spiral Review (1.OA.4, 1.OA.6)

3. Write the doubles plus one fact for $7 + 7$.

___ + ___ = ___

4. Write the doubles minus one fact for $4 + 4$.

___ + ___ = ___

5. Think of an addition fact to help you subtract.

$$\begin{array}{r} 14 \\ -9 \\ \hline \end{array}$$

$$\begin{array}{r} 9 \\ +\ \square \\ \hline 14 \end{array}$$

Name _____

Algebra • Equal and Not Equal

COMMON CORE STANDARD—1.OA.7
Work with addition and subtraction equations.

Which are true? Circle your answers.
Which are false? Cross out your answers.

1. $6 + 4 = 5 + 5$ 2. $10 = 6 - 4$ 3. $8 + 8 = 16 - 8$

4. $14 = 1 + 4$ 5. $8 - 0 = 12 - 4$ 6. $17 = 9 + 8$

7. $8 + 3 = 8 - 3$ 8. $15 - 6 = 6 + 9$ 9. $12 = 5 + 5 + 2$

10. $7 + 6 = 6 + 7$ 11. $5 - 4 = 4 + 5$ 12. $0 + 9 = 9 - 0$

Problem Solving Real World

13. Which are true? Use a to color.

$15 = 15$	$12 = 2$	$3 = 8 - 5$
$15 = 1 + 5$	$9 + 2 = 2 + 9$	$9 + 2 = 14$
$1 + 2 + 3 = 3 + 3$	$5 - 3 = 5 + 3$	$13 = 8 + 5$

Lesson Check (1.OA.7)

1. Circle the number sentences that are true.
Cross out the ones that are false.

$$4 + 3 = 9 - 2 \qquad\qquad 4 + 3 = 9 + 2$$

$$4 + 3 = 4 - 3 \qquad\qquad 4 + 3 = 6 + 1$$

Spiral Review (1.OA.2, 1.OA.6)

2. Use 5, 6 and 11 to write related
addition and subtraction sentences.

___ $\oplus$ ___ $=$ ___

___ $\oplus$ ___ $=$ ___

___ $\ominus$ ___ $=$ ___

___ $\ominus$ ___ $=$ ___

3. Solve. Draw or write to show your work.
Leah has 4 green toys, 5 pink toys,
and 2 blue toys. How many toys does Leah have?

_____ toys

Name _____

Facts Practice to 20

COMMON CORE STANDARD—1.OA.6
Add and subtract within 20.

Add or subtract.

1. $\quad 4$
$\quad + 9$

2. $\quad 13$
$\quad - 6$

3. $\quad 4$
$\quad + 5$

4. $\quad 8$
$\quad + 7$

5. $\quad 11$
$\quad - 6$

6. $\quad 17$
$\quad - 8$

7. $\quad 5$
$\quad + 7$

8. $\quad 13$
$\quad - 5$

9. $\quad 16$
$\quad - 9$

10. $\quad 3$
$\quad + 8$

11. $\quad 9$
$\quad - 8$

12. $\quad 7$
$\quad + 6$

13. $\quad 9$
$\quad - \square$
$\quad 7$

14. $\quad 6$
$\quad + \square$
$\quad 10$

15. $\quad 8$
$\quad - \square$
$\quad 3$

16. $\quad 6$
$\quad + \square$
$\quad 12$

17. $\quad 0$
$\quad + \square$
$\quad 9$

18. $\quad 15$
$\quad - \square$
$\quad 6$

Problem Solving

Solve. Draw or write to explain.

19. Kara has 9 drawings.
She gives 4 away. How many
drawings does Kara have now?

_____ drawings

Lesson Check (1.OA.6)

1. Add or subtract.

$$\begin{array}{r} 14 \\ -\ 7 \\ \hline \end{array} \qquad \begin{array}{r} 15 \\ -\ 6 \\ \hline \end{array} \qquad \begin{array}{r} 8 \\ +\ 7 \\ \hline \end{array} \qquad \begin{array}{r} 5 \\ +\ 8 \\ \hline \end{array}$$

Spiral Review (1.OA.3, 1.OA.8)

2. What is the missing number?
Write the missing addend.

$$7 + \square = 12$$

3. Greg knows $7 + 4 = 11$. What other
addition fact does he know that
shows the same addends?
Write the new fact.

___ + ___ = ___

School-Home Letter

Dear Family,

My class started Chapter 6 this week. In this chapter, I will count numbers to 120 and use tens and ones to make numbers.

Love, _____

Vocabulary

ones and **ten** You can group 10 to make 1 ten.

10 ones = 1 ten

hundred 10 tens is the same as 1 hundred.

10 tens = 100

Home Activity

Give your child a handful of craft sticks, chenille stems, or straws. Have your child make as many groups of 10 as possible, tying bundles of 10 with a rubber band. Have them place the bundles on a desk or table. Have your child put any leftover ones next to the bundles of 10. Then ask your child to write the number.

Literature

Reading math stories reinforces ideas. Look for these books in a library and read them with your child.

One Is a Snail, Ten Is a Crab by April Pulley Sayre. Candlewick, 2006.

The Counting Family by Jane Manners. Harcourt School Publishers, 2002.

Carta para la casa

Querida familia:

Mi clase comenzó el Capítulo 6 esta semana. En este capítulo, contaré números hasta el 120 y usaré decenas y unidades para formar números.

Con cariño, _____

Vocabulario

unidades y decenas puedes agrupar unidades para formar decenas

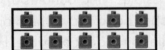

10 unidades = 1 decenas

centena 10 decenas es lo mismo que 1 centena

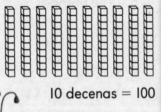

10 decenas = 100

Actividad para la casa

Entréguele a su hijo un puñado de palitos para manualidades, hilos de lana o pajitas. Pídale a su hijo que forme la mayor cantidad de grupos posible, atando paquetes de 10 con una banda elástica. Pídale que coloque los paquetes sobre un escritorio o mesa. Pídale que ponga las unidades sobrantes junto a los paquetes de 10. Luego, pídale a su hijo que escriba el número.

Literatura

Leer cuentos de matemáticas refuerza los conceptos. Busque estos libros en una biblioteca y léalos con su hijo.

One Is a Snail, Ten is a Crab
por April Pulley Sayre. Candlewick, 2006.

The Counting Family
por Jane Manners. Harcourt School Publishers, 2002.

Count by Ones to 120

COMMON CORE STANDARD—1.NBT.1
Extend the counting sequence.

Use a Counting Chart. Count forward. Write the numbers.

1. 40, ___, ___, ___, ___, ___, ___, ___, ___

2. 55, ___, ___, ___, ___, ___, ___, ___, ___

3. 37, ___, ___, ___, ___, ___, ___, ___, ___

4. 102, ___, ___, ___, ___, ___, ___, ___, ___

5. 96, ___, ___, ___, ___, ___, ___, ___, ___

Problem Solving Real World

Use a Counting Chart. Draw and write numbers to solve.

6. The bag has 111 marbles. Draw more marbles so there are 117 marbles in all. Write the numbers as you count.

Lesson Check (1.NBT.1)

1. Count forward. Write the
missing number.

$$110, 111, 112, \underline{\hspace{1cm}}, 114$$

Spiral Review (1.OA.1)

2. Solve. Write the number.
There are 6 bees. 2 bees fly
away. How many bees
are there now?

_____ bees

3. Solve. Draw a model to explain.
There are 8 children. 6 children
are boys. The rest are girls.
How many children are girls?

_____ girls

Count by Tens to 120

COMMON CORE STANDARD—1.NBT.1
Extend the counting sequence.

Use a Counting Chart.
Count by tens.
Write the numbers.

1. 1, ____, ____, ____, ____, ____, ____, ____, ____

2. 14, ____, ____, ____, ____, ____, ____, ____, ____

3. 7, ____, ____, ____, ____, ____, ____, ____, ____

4. 29, ____, ____, ____, ____, ____, ____, ____, ____

5. 5, ____, ____, ____, ____, ____, ____, ____, ____

6. 12, ____, ____, ____, ____, ____, ____, ____, ____

7. 26, ____, ____, ____, ____, ____, ____, ____, ____

8. 3, ____, ____, ____, ____, ____, ____, ____, ____

9. 8, ____, ____, ____, ____, ____, ____, ____, ____

Problem Solving

Solve.

10. I am after 70.
I am before 90.
You say me when you count by tens.
What number am I?

____

Lesson Check (1.NBT.1)

1. Count by tens.
Write the missing numbers.

$$44, 54, 64, \rule{1.5cm}{0.4pt}, \rule{1.5cm}{0.4pt}, 94$$

Spiral Review (1.OA.6)

2. Use the model. Write to show
how you make a ten. Then add.

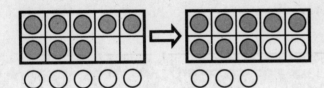

___ + ___ + ___

___ + ___ = ___

So, ___ + ___ = ___

3. Write a number sentence
to complete the related facts.

$9 + 6 = 15$ $15 - 6 = 9$

$6 + 9 = 15$

Understand Ten and Ones

COMMON CORE STANDARD—1.NBT.2b
Understand place value.

Use the model. Write the number three different ways.

1.

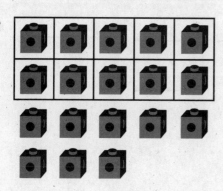

_____ ten _____ ones

_____ + _____

_____

2.

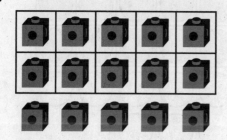

_____ ten _____ ones

_____ + _____

_____

Draw cubes to show the number.
Write the number different ways.

Rob has 7 ones. Nick has 5 ones. They put all their ones together. What number did they make?

3.

_____ ten _____ ones

_____ + _____

_____

Lesson Check (1.NBT.2b)

1. Use the model. Write the number three different ways.

____ ten ____ ones

____ + ____ = ____

____

· ·

Spiral Review (1.OA.6)

2. Use the model. Write the addition sentence. What number sentence does this model show?

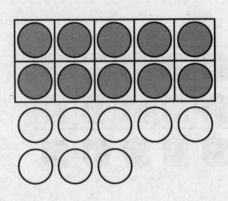

____ + ____ = ____

· ·

3. Write two subtraction facts related to $7 + 5 = 12$.

____ − ____ = ____

____ − ____ = ____

Make Ten and Ones

Use [cube]. Make groups of ten and ones. Draw your work. Write how many.

COMMON CORE STANDARD—1.NBT.2b
Understand place value.

1.

14
fourteen
____ ten ____ ones

2.

12
twelve
____ ten ____ ones

3.

15
fifteen
____ ten ____ ones

4.

18
eighteen
____ ten ____ ones

5.

11
eleven
____ ten ____ one

Problem Solving

Solve.

6. Tina thinks of a number that has 3 ones and 1 ten. What is the number?

____

Lesson Check (1.NBT.2b)

1. How many tens and ones make 17?
   Write the numbers.

17
seventeen

____ ten ____ ones

Spiral Review (1.OA.1, 1.OA.6)

2. Use the model. Write the
   addition sentence. What
   number sentence does
   this model show?

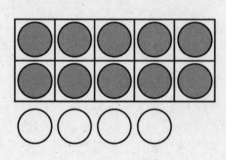

___ + ___ = ___

---

3. Choose a way to solve.
   Draw or write to explain.
   Ben has 17 books. He gives
   some away. He has 8 left.
   How many books does
   he give away?

____ books

Tens

Use [die]. Make groups of ten.
Write the tens and ones.

**COMMON CORE STANDARDS—1.NBT.2a,
1.NBT.2c** *Understand place value.*

I. 90 ones

_____ tens = _____ ones

_____ tens = _____
ninety

2. 50 ones

_____ tens = _____ ones

_____ tens = _____
fifty

3. 40 ones

_____ tens = _____ ones

_____ tens = _____
forty

4. 80 ones

_____ tens = _____ ones

_____ tens = _____
eighty

Problem Solving

Look at the model. Write the number.

5. What number does the model show?

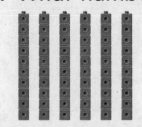

_____

Lesson Check (1.NBT.2a, 1.NBT.2c)

1. What number does the model show?
Write the number.

_____ tens = _____

2. What number does the model show?
Write the number.

_____ tens = _____

Spiral Review (1.OA.3, 1.OA.8)

3. Write the missing number.

$$6 + \boxed{} = 13$$

4. What is the sum for $3 + 3 + 4$?

_____

Name _____

Tens and Ones to 50

COMMON CORE STANDARDS—1.NBT.2
Understand place value.

Write the numbers.

1.

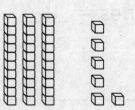

____ tens ____ ones = ____

2.

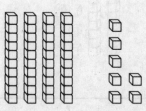

____ tens ____ ones = ____

3.

____ tens ____ ones = ____

4.

____ tens ____ ones = ____

Problem Solving Real World

Solve. Write the numbers.

5. I have 43 cubes. How many tens and ones can I make?

____ tens ____ ones

1. What number does the model show?
Write the numbers.

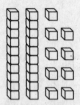

_____ tens _____ ones = _____

2. What number does the model show?
Write the numbers.

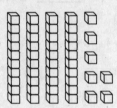

_____ tens _____ ones = _____

Spiral Review (1.OA.1, 1.OA.6)

3. Write the sum?

$$6$$
$$+\underline{3}$$

4. Show taking from. Circle the
part you take from the group.
Then cross it out.
Write the difference.

$$6 - 4 = \underline{}$$

Tens and Ones to 100

COMMON CORE STANDARDS—1.NBT.2
Understand place value.

Write the numbers.

1.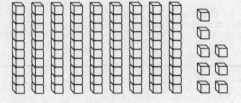

_____ tens _____ ones = _____

2.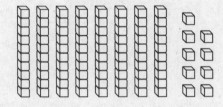

_____ tens _____ ones = _____

3.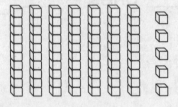

_____ tens _____ ones = _____

4.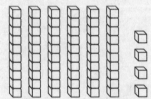

_____ tens _____ ones = _____

Problem Solving Real World

Draw a quick picture to show the number.
Write how many tens and ones there are.

5. Inez has 57 shells.

_____ tens _____ ones

Lesson Check (1.NBT.2)

1. What number has 10 tens 0 ones?

_____

2. What number does
the model show?
Write the numbers.

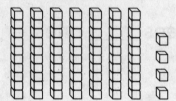

_____ tens _____ ones = _____

....

Spiral Review (1.OA.3, 1.OA.5)

3. Barry knows that $6 + 5 = 11$.
What other addition fact does
he know? Write the new fact.

_____ + _____ = _____

....

4. Count on to solve $2 + 6$.
Write the sum.

$2 + 6 =$ _____

Name _____

Problem Solving • Show Numbers in Different Ways

COMMON CORE STANDARDS—1.NBT.2A, 1.NBT.3 *Understand place value.*

Use ▭ ▭ to show the number two different ways. Draw both ways.

1. 62

Tens	Ones

___ ◯ ___

Tens	Ones

2. 38

Tens	Ones

___ ◯ ___

Tens	Ones

3. 47

Tens	Ones

___ ◯ ___

Tens	Ones

Lesson Check (1.NBT.2a, 1.NBT.3)

1. What number does each model show? Write the numbers.

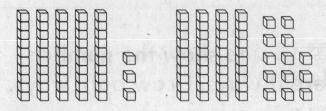

___ = ___

2. What number does the model show? Write the number.

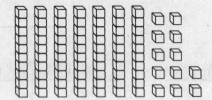

___

Spiral Review (1.OA.6)

3. Subtract to solve. Then add to check your answer.

$12 - 4 = \boxed{}$

$\boxed{} + 4 = \boxed{}$

4. Write two ways to make 15.

$15 = \underline{} + \underline{}$ $15 = \underline{} + \underline{}$

Model, Read, and Write Numbers from 100 to 110

COMMON CORE STANDARDS—1.NBT.1
Understand place value.

Use ▭ ▫ to show the number.
Write the number.

1. 10 tens and
6 more

_____

2. 10 tens and
1 more

_____

3. 10 tens and
9 more

_____

Write the number.

4.

5.

_____

_____

Problem Solving Real World

6. Solve to find the number of pens.

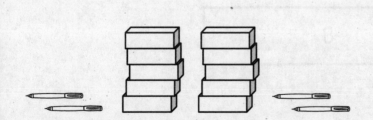

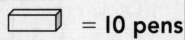

THINK
✎ = 1 pen
▭ = 10 pens

There are _____ pens.

Lesson Check (1.NBT.1)

1. What number does the model show?
   Write the number.

_____

....

Spiral Review (1.OA.1)

2. Show taking from. Circle the
   part you take from the group.
   Then cross it out.
   Write the difference.

$4 - 3 = \underline{\quad}$

....

3. Use the model to solve. Ken has
   8 pennies. Ron has 3 pennies.
   How many fewer pennies does
   Ron have than Ken?

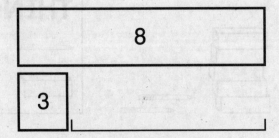

_____

Name _____

Model, Read, and Write Numbers from 110 to 120

COMMON CORE STANDARDS—1.NBT.1
Extend the counting sequence.

Use ▭ to model the number.
Write the number.

1.

_____

2.

_____

3.

_____

4.

_____

5.

_____

6.

_____

Problem Solving Real World

Choose a way to solve. Draw or write to explain.

7. Dave collects rocks. He makes 12 groups of 10 rocks and has none left over. How many rocks does Dave have?

_____ rocks

Lesson Check (1.NBT.1)

1. What number does the model show?
   Write the number.

   ___

....

Spiral Review (1.OA.6)

2. Show how to make a ten to solve 13 − 7.
   Write the number sentence.

Step 1   Step 2

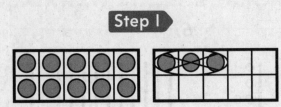   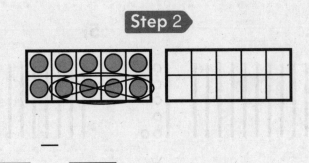

   ___ − ___ ___

   ___ − ___ = ___

   So, 13 − 7 = ___.

....

3. What is the difference?
   Write the number.

$$\begin{array}{r} 9 \\ -\,4 \\ \hline \end{array}$$

School-Home Letter

Dear Family,

My class started Chapter 7 this week. In this chapter, I will compare numbers to show greater than or less than. I will also use <, >, and = to compare numbers.

Love, _____

Vocabulary

is greater than > a symbol used to show that a number is greater than another number

$$11 > 10$$
11 is greater than 10

is less than < a symbol used to show that a number is less than another number

$$10 < 11$$
10 is less than 11

Home Activity

Make flash cards for the greater than symbol >, and the less than symbol <. Each day, choose two numbers between 1 and 100. Use the flashcards with your child to compare the numbers.

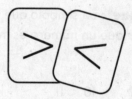

Literature

Look for these books in a library. Use < and > flashcards to compare the groups of objects.

Just Enough Carrots by Stuart J. Murphy. HarperTrophy, 1997.

More, Fewer, Less by Tana Hoban. Greenwillow, 1998.

Carta para la casa

Querida familia:

Mi clase comenzó el Capítulo 7 esta semana. En este capítulo, compararé números para mostrar los conceptos de mayor que y menor que. También usaré los símbolos <, >, e = para comparar números.

Con cariño, _____

Vocabulario

es mayor que > un símbolo que se usa para mostrar que un número es mayor que otro número

$$11 > 10$$
11 es mayor que 10

es menor que < un símbolo que se usa para mostrar que un número es menor que otro número

$$10 < 11$$
10 es menor que 11

Actividad para la casa

Haga tarjetas nemotécnicas con el símbolo es mayor que > y el símbolo es menor que <. Cada día, elija dos números entre 1 y 100. Use las tarjetas nemotécnicas con su hijo para comparar los números.

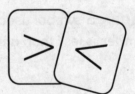

Literatura

Busque estos libros en una biblioteca. Use tarjetas nemotécnicas con < y > para comparar grupos de objetos.

Just Enough Carrots
por Stuart J. Murphy. Harper Collins, 1997.

More, Fewer, Less
por Tana Hoban. Greenwillow, 1998.

Algebra • Greater Than

COMMON CORE STANDARDS—1.NBT.3
Understand place value.

Use ▭ ▭ if you need to.

Circle the greater number.	Did tens or ones help you decide?	Write the numbers.
1. 22　42	tens　ones	____ is greater than ____. ____ > ____
2. 46　64	tens　ones	____ is greater than ____. ____ > ____
3. 88　86	tens　ones	____ is greater than ____. ____ > ____
4. 92　29	tens　ones	____ is greater than ____. ____ > ____

Problem Solving Real World

5. Color the blocks that show numbers greater than 47.

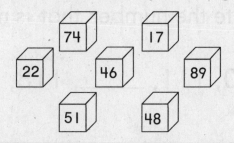

Lesson Check (1.NBT.3)

1. Circle the number that is greater than 65.
Write the numbers.

37   49   56   66

_____ is greater than _____.

_____ > _____

2. Circle the number that is greater than 29.
Write the numbers.

19   20   28   92

_____ is greater than _____.

_____ > _____

Spiral Review (1.OA.6, 1.NBT.1)

3. What is $5 + 7$? Write the sum.

$5 + 7 =$ _____

4. Count forward. Write the number that is missing.

110, 111, _____, 113, 114

Algebra • Less Than

COMMON CORE STANDARD—1.NBT.3
Understand place value.

Use ▭▭▭▭ ▯ if you need to.

Circle the number that is less.	Did tens or ones help you decide?	Write the numbers.
1. 34 36	tens ones	____ is less than ____. ____ < ____
2. 75 57	tens ones	____ is less than ____. ____ < ____
3. 80 89	tens ones	____ is less than ____. ____ < ____
4. 13 31	tens ones	____ is less than ____. ____ < ____

Problem Solving

Write a number to solve.

5. Lori makes the number 74. Gabe makes
a number that is less than 74. What
could be a number Gabe makes? ____

Lesson Check (1.NBT.3)

I. Circle the number that is less than 52.
Write the numbers.

25   52   64   88

___ is less than ___.

___ < ___

---

2. Circle the number that is less than 76.
Write the numbers.

100   81   77   59

___ is less than ___.

___ < ___

Spiral Review (1.NBT.1, 1.NBT.2)

3. Write the number. What number
does the model show?

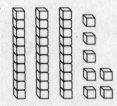

____ tens and ____ ones = ____

4. Count by tens.
Write the missing numbers.

8, 18, 28, ____, ____, 58

Algebra • Use Symbols to Compare

COMMON CORE STANDARD—1.NBT.3
Understand place value.

Write $<$, $>$, or $=$.
Draw a quick picture if you need to.

1.

38 ◯ 31

2.

26 ◯ 42

3. 88 ◯ 78

4. 77 ◯ 77

5. 91 ◯ 89

6. 80 ◯ 82

7. 33 ◯ 44

8. 51 ◯ 60

9. 70 ◯ 70

10. 99 ◯ 98

11. 85 ◯ 58

Problem Solving

Write $<$, $>$, or $=$ to solve. Circle your answer.

12. Tracey has 26 pennies. Heba has
29 pennies. Who has a greater
number of pennies?

Tracey   Heba

29 ◯ 26

Lesson Check (1.NBT.3)

1. Compare each pair of numbers. Write $<$, $>$, or $=$.

22 $\bigcirc$ 28 ┊ 28 $\bigcirc$ 28 ┊ 22 $\bigcirc$ 22 ┊ 28 $\bigcirc$ 22

2. Compare each pair of numbers. Write $<$, $>$, or $=$.

78 $\bigcirc$ 87 ┊ 78 $\bigcirc$ 78 ┊ 87 $\bigcirc$ 78 ┊ 87 $\bigcirc$ 87

Spiral Review (1.NBT.2, 1.NBT.2b)

3. What number does the
model show?
Write the numbers.

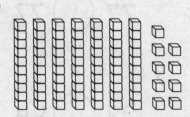

_____ tens and _____ ones = _____

4. Use the model. Write the
number three different ways.

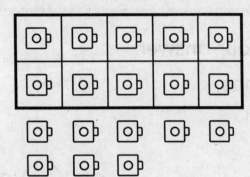

_____ ten _____ ones

_____ + _____

_____

Problem Solving •
Compare Numbers

COMMON CORE STANDARD—1.NBT.3
Understand place value.

Make a model to solve.

1. Ava has these number cards. She gives away cards with numbers less than 34 and greater than 38. Which number cards does Ava have now?

   | 32 | 33 | 35 | 37 | 39 |

   Ava has number cards _____.

2. Ron has these number cards. He keeps the cards with numbers greater than 60 and less than 56. Circle the number cards Ron keeps.

   | 54 | 57 | 58 | 59 | 61 |

   Ron keeps number cards _____.

3. Mia has these number cards. She keeps the cards with numbers less than 85 and greater than 88. Circle the cards Mia keeps.

   | 84 | 86 | 87 | 89 | 90 |

   Mia keeps number cards _____.

Lesson Check (1.NBT.3)

I. Juan crosses out the numbers that are less than 45 and greater than 50. Circle the numbers that are left.

| 43 | 44 | 46 | 49 | 52 |

Spiral Review (1.OA.5, 1.OA.6)

2. Count back 3.
   Write is the difference.

$$9 - 3 = \underline{\hspace{1cm}}$$

3. Write the number to complete the related facts.

$$4 + 7 = 11 \qquad 11 - 4 = 7$$
$$7 + 4 = 11 \qquad \underline{\hspace{0.8cm}} - \underline{\hspace{0.8cm}} = \underline{\hspace{0.8cm}}$$

10 Less, 10 More

COMMON CORE STANDARD—1.NBT.5
Use place value understanding and properties of operations to add and subtract.

Use mental math.
Complete the chart.

	10 Less		**10 More**
1.	____	48	____
2.	____	25	____
3.	____	73	____
4.	____	89	____
5.	8	____	____
6.	____	____	47

Problem Solving Real World

Choose a way to solve. Draw or write to show your work.

7. Jim has 16 pennies. Doug has 10 fewer pennies than Jim. How many pennies does Doug have?

____ pennies

Lesson Check (1.NBT.5)

1. What number is 10 less than 67.
Write the number.

_____

2. What number is 10 more than 39.
Write the number.

_____

Spiral Review (1.NBT.2b, 1.NBT.2c)

3. How many tens and ones
make this number?
Write how many.

_____ ten _____ ones

18
eighteen

4. Look at the model. Write the number.
What number does the model show?

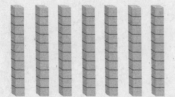

_____ tens = _____

School-Home Letter

Dear Family,

My class started Chapter 8 this week. In this chapter, I will learn how to add and subtract two-digit numbers.

Love, _____

Vocabulary

ones and tens You can group ones to make tens.

20 ones = 2 tens

Home Activity

Using a jar and pennies, work with your child to add and subtract two-digit numbers. Start with 11 pennies in the jar. Have your child add 13 pennies. Ask your child to explain a way to find the sum of 11 and 13. Then count with your child to find how many pennies in all. Repeat with different quantities each day. Work with your child to subtract numbers as well.

Literature

Reading math stories reinforces ideas. Look for these books in a library and read them with your child.

One Is a Snail, Ten Is a Crab
by April Pulley Sayre. Candlewick, 2006.

Safari Park
by Stuart J. Murphy. Steck-Vaughn, 2002.

Carta para la casa

Querida familia:

Mi clase comenzó el Capítulo 8 esta semana. En este capítulo, aprenderé a sumar y restar números de dos dígitos.

Con cariño, _____

Vocabulario

unidades y decenas Puedes agrupar unidades para formar decenas.

20 unidades = 2 decenas

Actividad para la casa

Con un tarro y centavos, trabaje con su hijo para sumar y restar números de dos dígitos. Comience con 11 monedas de 1¢ en el tarro. Pídale que sume 13 monedas de 1¢. Pídale que explique cómo encontrar la suma de 11 y 13. Luego, cuente con su hijo para saber cuántos centavos hay en total. Repita con diferentes cantidades cada día. Trabaje con él para restar números también.

Literatura

Leer cuentos de matemáticas refuerza las ideas. Busque estos libros en la biblioteca y léalos con su hijo.

One Is a Snail, Ten Is a Crab
por April Pulley Sayre. Candlewick, 2006.

Safari Park
por Stuart J. Murphy. Steck-Vaughn, 2002.

Add and Subtract within 20

COMMON CORE STANDARD—1.OA.6
Add and subtract within 20.

Add or subtract.

1. $6 + 0$

2. $11 - 2$

3. $4 + 5$

4. $9 + 8$

5. $4 + 10$

6. $14 - 9$

7. $7 + 4$

8. $8 - 5$

9. $12 - 3$

10. $6 + 7$

11. $18 - 9$

12. $15 - 6$

13. $6 + 5$

14. $12 - 6$

15. $10 - 10$

16. $13 - 7$

17. $2 + 7$

18. $6 + 4$

Problem Solving

Solve. Draw or write to explain.

19. Jesse has 4 shells. He finds some more. Now he has 12 shells. How many more shells did Jesse find?

_____ more shells

Lesson Check (1.OA.6)

1. What is the sum?
Write the number.

$$8 + 5 = \underline{\quad}$$

2. What is the difference?
Write the number.

$$11 - 4 = \underline{\quad}$$

Spiral Review (1.NBT.3)

3.

Circle the greater number.	Did tens or ones help you decide?	Write the numbers.
43 46	tens ones	_____ is greater than _____. _____ > _____

4.

Circle the number that is less.	Did tens or ones help you decide?	Write the numbers.
69 84	tens ones	_____ is less than _____. _____ < _____

Add Tens

COMMON CORE STANDARD—1.NBT.4
Use place value understanding and properties
of operations to add and subtract.

Draw to show tens. Write the sum.
Write how many tens.

1. $10 + 30 =$ ___

___ tens

2. $30 + 30 =$ ___

___ tens

3. $60 + 10 =$ ___

___ tens

4. $20 + 20 =$ ___

___ tens

5. $30 + 20 =$ ___

___ tens

6. $10 + 70 =$ ___

___ tens

Problem Solving

Draw tens to solve.

7. Drew makes 20 posters. Tia makes
30 posters. How many posters do
they make?

___ posters

8. Regina read 40 pages. Alice
read 50 pages. How many
pages did they read?

___ pages

Lesson Check (1.NBT.4)

1. What is the sum?
Write the number.

$$20 + 30 = \underline{\quad}$$

2. What is the sum?
Write the number.

$$30 + 10 = \underline{\quad}$$

Spiral Review (1.OA.6, 1.NBT.3)

3. Write a doubles fact that can help you solve $6 + 5 = 11$.

$$\underline{\quad} + \underline{\quad} = \underline{\quad}$$

4. Circle the number sentences that are true.
Cross out the number sentences that are false.
Which is **not** true?

$$30 > 10 \qquad 30 < 10 \qquad 10 > 30 \qquad 10 < 30$$

Name _____

Subtract Tens

Draw to show tens. Write the difference. Write how many tens.

COMMON CORE STANDARD—1.NBT.6
Use place value understanding and properties of operations to add and subtract.

1. $40 - 10 =$ ____

____ tens

2. $80 - 40 =$ ____

____ tens

3. $50 - 30 =$ ____

____ tens

4. $60 - 30 =$ ____

____ tens

Problem Solving

Draw tens to solve.

5. Mario has 70 baseball cards.
He gives 30 to Lisa.
How many baseball cards
does Mario have left?

____ baseball cards

Lesson Check (1.NBT.6)

1. What is the difference?
Write the number.

$$60 - 20 = \underline{\hspace{1cm}}$$

2. What is the difference?
Write the number.

$$70 - 30 = \underline{\hspace{1cm}}$$

Spiral Review (1.OA.6, 1.NBT.3)

3. Use ○, ●, and a ten frame. Show
both addends. Draw to make ten.
Then write a new fact. Add.

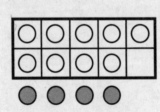
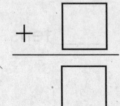
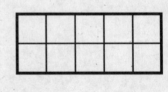

4. Bo crosses out the number cards that are
less than 33 and greater than 38.
What numbers are left?

| 30 | 32 | 36 | 37 | 39 |

Number cards _____ and _____ are left.

Use a Hundred Chart to Add

COMMON CORE STANDARD—1.NBT.4
Use place value understanding and properties of operations to add and subtract.

**Use the hundred chart to add.
Count on by ones or tens.**

1. $47 + 2 =$ _____

2. $26 + 50 =$ _____

3. $22 + 5 =$ _____

4. $40 + 41 =$ _____

5. $4 + 85 =$ _____

1	2	3	4	5	6	7	8	9	10
11	12	13	14	15	16	17	18	19	20
21	22	23	24	25	26	27	28	29	30
31	32	33	34	35	36	37	38	39	40
41	42	43	44	45	46	47	48	49	50
51	52	53	54	55	56	57	58	59	60
61	62	63	64	65	66	67	68	69	70
71	72	73	74	75	76	77	78	79	80
81	82	83	84	85	86	87	88	89	90
91	92	93	94	95	96	97	98	99	100

Problem Solving

Choose a way to solve. Draw or write to show your work.

6. 17 children are on the bus. Then 20 more children get on the bus. How many children are on the bus now?

_____ children

Lesson Check (1.NBT.4)

1. What is the sum?
Write the number.

$$42 + 50 = \underline{}$$

_____

2. What is the sum?
Write the number.

$$11 + 8 = \underline{}$$

1	2	3	4	5	6	7	8	9	10
11	12	13	14	15	16	17	18	19	20
21	22	23	24	25	26	27	28	29	30
31	32	33	34	35	36	37	38	39	40
41	42	43	44	45	46	47	48	49	50
51	52	53	54	55	56	57	58	59	60
61	62	63	64	65	66	67	68	69	70
71	72	73	74	75	76	77	78	79	80
81	82	83	84	85	86	87	88	89	90
91	92	93	94	95	96	97	98	99	100

Spiral Review (1.OA.8, 1.NBT.5)

3. Use mental math.
What number is ten less than 52?
Write the number.

$$\underline{}$$

4. Write an addition fact that helps
you solve 16 − 9.

$$\underline{} + \underline{} = \underline{}$$

Use Models to Add

COMMON CORE STANDARD—1.NBT.4
Use place value understanding and properties of operations to add and subtract.

Use ⬜⬜⬜⬜⬜⬜ ⬜ and your MathBoard.
Add the ones or tens. Write the sum.

1. $44 + 5 =$ ___

2. $16 + 70 =$ ___

3. $78 + 20 =$ ___

4. $52 + 7 =$ ___

5. $2 + 13 =$ ___

6. $73 + 4 =$ ___

7. $84 + 3 =$ ___

8. $20 + 25 =$ ___

9. $49 + 30 =$ ___

10. $81 + 8 =$ ___

Problem Solving

Solve. Draw or write to explain.

11. Maria has 21 marbles.
    She buys a bag of 20 marbles.
    How many marbles does
    Maria have now?

    ___ marbles

Lesson Check (1.NBT.4)

1. What is the sum?
   Write the number.

$$62 + 30 = \underline{\quad}$$

2. What is the sum?
   Write the number.

$$37 + 2 = \underline{\quad}$$

Spiral Review (1.OA.6, 1.NBT.1)

3. Write two ways to make 15.

   $$\underline{\quad} + \underline{\quad} = 15$$

   $$\underline{\quad} + \underline{\quad} = 15$$

4. What number does the model show?

$$\underline{\quad}$$

P146 one hundred forty-six

Make Ten to Add

COMMON CORE STANDARD—1.NBT.4
Use place value understanding and properties
of operations to add and subtract.

Use ▭▭▭. Draw to show how you make a ten. Find the sum.

1. $26 + 5 = $ _____

2. $68 + 4 = $ _____

3. $35 + 8 = $ _____

Problem Solving Real World

Choose a way to solve. Draw or write to show your work.

4. Debbie has 27 markers. Sal has 9 markers. How many markers do they have?

_____ markers

Lesson Check (1.NBT.4)

1. What is the sum?
   Write the number.

$$47 + 6 = \underline{}$$

2. What is the sum?
   Write the number.

$$84 + 8 = \underline{}$$

Spiral Review (1.OA.7, 1.NBT.1)

3. What number does the
   model show?
   Write the number.

$$\underline{}$$

4. Write a number to make the sentence true.

$$5 + 4 = 10 - \underline{}$$

Use Place Value to Add

COMMON CORE STANDARD—1.NBT.4
Use place value understanding and properties of operations to add and subtract.

Draw a quick picture. Use tens and ones to add.

1.

$$\begin{array}{r} 31 \\ + 26 \\ \hline \end{array}$$

Tens	Ones

3 tens + 1 one
2 tens + 6 ones
_____

___ tens + ___ ones

___ + ___ = ___

$$\begin{array}{r} 31 \\ + 26 \\ \hline \end{array}$$

2.

$$\begin{array}{r} 54 \\ + 34 \\ \hline \end{array}$$

Tens	Ones

5 tens + 4 ones
3 tens + 4 ones
_____

___ tens + ___ ones

___ + ___ = ___

$$\begin{array}{r} 54 \\ + 34 \\ \hline \end{array}$$

Problem Solving Real World

3. Write two addition sentences you can use to find the sum. Then solve.

Addend   **Addend**

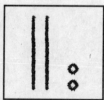

___ + ___ = ___

___ + ___ = ___

Lesson Check (1.NBT.4)

1. What is the sum?
   Write the number.

$$42 \\ +\ 31$$

2. What is the sum?
   Write the number.

$$23 \\ +\ 12$$

Spiral Review (1.OA.6, 1.NBT.2)

3. I have 28 cubes. How many tens and ones can I make?

   _____ tens _____ ones

   _____ ten _____ ones

4. What is the sum?
   Write the number.

$$5 \\ +\ 5$$

P150 one hundred fifty

© Houghton Mifflin Harcourt Publishing Company

Problem Solving • Addition Word Problems

COMMON CORE STANDARD—1.NBT.4
Use place value understanding and properties of operations to add and subtract.

Draw and write to solve. Explain your reasoning.

1. Dale saved 19 pennies. Then he found 5 more pennies. How many pennies does Dale have now?

   _____

   _____

   _____ pennies

2. Jean has 10 fish. She gets 4 more fish. How many fish does she have now?

   _____

   _____

   _____ fish

3. Courtney buys 2 bags of apples. Each bag has 20 apples. How many apples does she buy?

   _____

   _____

   _____ apples

4. John bakes 18 blueberry muffins and 12 banana muffins for the bake sale. How many muffins does he bake?

   _____

   _____

   _____ muffins

Lesson Check (1.NBT.4)

1. Amy has 9 books about dogs.
   She has 13 books about cats.
   How many books does she
   have about dogs and cats?
   Solve. Show your work. Write the number. _____ books

Spiral Review (1.OA.3, 1.OA.6)

2. What is the sum for $4 + 2 + 4$?
   Write the number.

   _____

3. Solve. Use the ten frame to make a
   ten to help you subtract. Ray has
   14 pens. 8 are black. The rest
   are blue. How many pens are blue? _____ blue pens

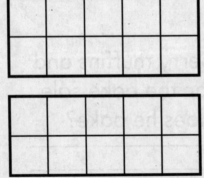

Related Addition and Subtraction

COMMON CORE STANDARDS—1.NBT.4,
1.NBT.6 Use place value understanding and
properties of operations to add and subtract.

Use the hundred chart to add and subtract. Count up and back by tens.

1. $16 + 60 =$ _____

   $76 - 60 =$ _____

2. $61 + 30 =$ _____

   $91 - 30 =$ _____

3. $64 + 20 =$ _____

   $84 - 20 =$ _____

1	2	3	4	5	6	7	8	9	10
11	12	13	14	15	16	17	18	19	20
21	22	23	24	25	26	27	28	29	30
31	32	33	34	35	36	37	38	39	40
41	42	43	44	45	46	47	48	49	50
51	52	53	54	55	56	57	58	59	60
61	62	63	64	65	66	67	68	69	70
71	72	73	74	75	76	77	78	79	80
81	82	83	84	85	86	87	88	89	90
91	92	93	94	95	96	97	98	99	100

Problem Solving

Choose a way to solve. Draw or write to show your work.

4. There are 53 leaves in a tree. 20 leaves blow away. How many leaves are left in the tree?

   _____ leaves

Lesson Check

1. What is 78 − 20?
Write the number.

____

1	2	3	4	5	6	7	8	9	10
11	12	13	14	15	16	17	18	19	20
21	22	23	24	25	26	27	28	29	30
31	32	33	34	35	36	37	38	39	40
41	42	43	44	45	46	47	48	49	50
51	52	53	54	55	56	57	58	59	60
61	62	63	64	65	66	67	68	69	70
71	72	73	74	75	76	77	78	79	80
81	82	83	84	85	86	87	88	89	90
91	92	93	94	95	96	97	98	99	100

2. What is 37 + 50?
Write the number.

____

Spiral Review

3. Use the model.
What is the difference of 7 − 3?
Write the number.

$$7 - 3 = \underline{}$$

4. What is the sum for 0 + 7?
Write the number.

____

Name _____

Practice Addition and Subtraction

COMMON CORE STANDARDS—1.NBT.4, 1.NBT.6 Use place value understanding and properties of operations to add and subtract.

Add or subtract.

1. $\begin{array}{r} 20 \\ + 20 \\ \hline \end{array}$
2. $\begin{array}{r} 90 \\ - 30 \\ \hline \end{array}$
3. $\begin{array}{r} 52 \\ + 4 \\ \hline \end{array}$
4. $\begin{array}{r} 62 \\ + 21 \\ \hline \end{array}$
5. $\begin{array}{r} 39 \\ - 10 \\ \hline \end{array}$

6. $\begin{array}{r} 8 \\ + 2 \\ \hline \end{array}$
7. $\begin{array}{r} 47 \\ + 34 \\ \hline \end{array}$
8. $\begin{array}{r} 4 \\ - 0 \\ \hline \end{array}$
9. $\begin{array}{r} 49 \\ - 6 \\ \hline \end{array}$
10. $\begin{array}{r} 64 \\ + 30 \\ \hline \end{array}$

11. $\begin{array}{r} 63 \\ + 11 \\ \hline \end{array}$
12. $\begin{array}{r} 37 \\ - 6 \\ \hline \end{array}$
13. $\begin{array}{r} 85 \\ + 13 \\ \hline \end{array}$
14. $\begin{array}{r} 48 \\ + 11 \\ \hline \end{array}$
15. $\begin{array}{r} 76 \\ - 15 \\ \hline \end{array}$

Problem Solving

Solve. Write or draw to explain.

16. Andrew read 17 pages of his book before dinner. He read 9 more pages after dinner. How many pages did he read?

_____ pages

Lesson Check (1.NBT.4)

1. What is the sum of $20 + 18$?
   Write the sum.

$$20 + 18 = \underline{\hspace{1cm}}$$

2. What is the difference of $90 - 50$?
   Write the difference.

$$90 - 50 = \underline{\hspace{1cm}}$$

Spiral Review (1.OA.1, 1.OA.6)

3. Use the model. What number
   sentence does this model show?
   Write the number sentence that
   the model shows.

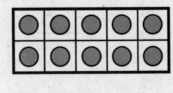

$$\underline{\hspace{0.8cm}} + \underline{\hspace{0.8cm}} = \underline{\hspace{0.8cm}}$$

4. Solve. Mo had some toys. He gave 6 away.
   Now he has 6 toys. How many toys did
   Mo start with?

$$\underline{\hspace{1cm}} \text{ toys}$$

School-Home Letter

Dear Family,

My class started Chapter 9 this week. In this chapter, I will learn about measurement. I will use length to compare, order, and measure objects. I will also use time to tell time to the hour and half hour.

Love, _____

Vocabulary

hour

half hour

Home Activity

Cut strips of paper in varying lengths and place them in random order on a table. Have children put the strips of paper in order from longest to shortest.

Literature

Look for these books in a library.

How Big Is a Foot?
Rolf Myller.
Dell Yearling, 1991.

Super Sand Castle Saturday
Stuart J. Murphy.
HarperTrophy, 1999.

Carta
para la casa

Querida familia:

Mi clase comenzó el Capítulo 9 esta semana. En este capítulo, aprenderé sobre medidas. Usaré la longitud para comparar, ordenar y medir objetos. También usaré el tiempo para decir la hora y la media hora.

Con cariño, _____

Vocabulario

hora

media hora

Actividad para la casa

Corte tiras de papel que tengan una longitud variada y colóquelas sobre una mesa en orden aleatorio. Pídales a los niños que pongan las tiras de papel en orden, de la más larga a la más corta.

Literatura

Busque estos libros en una biblioteca.

How Big Is a Foot?
por Rolf Myller.
Dell Yearling, 1991.

Sábado de super castillos
por Stuart J. Murphy.
HarperTrophy, 1998.

Order Length

COMMON CORE STANDARD—1.MD.1
Measure lengths indirectly and by iterating length units.

Draw three pencils in order from shortest to longest.

1. shortest

2.

3. longest

Draw three markers in order from longest to shortest.

4. longest

5.

6. shortest

Problem Solving Real World

Solve.

7. Fred has the shortest toothbrush in the bathroom. Circle Fred's toothbrush.

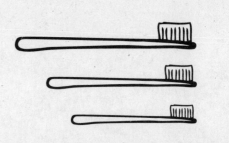

Lesson Check (1.MD.1)

1. Draw three crayons in order from longest to shortest.

2. Draw three paint brushes in order from shortest to longest.

Spiral Review (1.NBT.2a, 1.NBT.3)

3. Use ▭▭▭▭▭▭▭ ▯ to show 22 two different ways. Draw both ways.

Tens	Ones		Tens	Ones

Indirect Measurement

COMMON CORE STANDARD—1.MD.1
Measure lengths indirectly and by iterating length units.

Read the clues. Write shorter or longer to complete the sentence. Then draw to prove your answer.

1. Clue 1: A yarn is longer than a ribbon.
Clue 2: The ribbon is longer than a crayon.

So, the yarn is _____ than the crayon.

yarn

ribbon

crayon

Problem Solving *Real World*

Solve. Draw or write to explain.

2. Megan's pencil is shorter than Tasha's pencil.

Tasha's pencil is shorter than Kim's pencil.

Is Megan's pencil shorter or longer than Kim's pencil?

_____

_____

Lesson Check (1.MD.1)

1. A black line is longer than a
   gray line. The gray line is longer
   than a white line. Is the black
   line shorter or longer than the
   white line? Draw to prove your answer.

Spiral Review (1.NBT.4)

2. What is the sum?
   Write the number.

$$42 + 20 = \underline{\quad}$$

Name _____

Use Nonstandard Units to Measure Length

COMMON CORE STANDARD—1.MD.2
Measure lengths indirectly and by iterating
length units.

Use real objects. Use ▇ to measure.

1.

   about _____ ▇

2.

   about _____ ▇

3.

   about _____ ▇

4.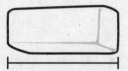

   about _____ ▇

Problem Solving Real World

Solve.

5. Don measures his desk with ▇.
   About how long is his desk?

   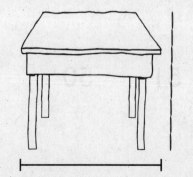

   about _____ ▇

one hundred sixty-three **P163**

Lesson Check (1.MD.2)

1. Use ■. Kevin measures the ribbon with ■.
About how long is the ribbon?

about ____ ■

....

Spiral Review (1.NBT.3, 1.NBT.4)

2. Draw and write to solve.
I have 27 red flowers and
19 white flowers. How many
flowers do I have?

____ flowers

....

3. Circle the number that is less.	Did tens or ones help you decide?	Write the numbers.
		____ is less than ____
51 50	tens ones	____ < ____

Make a Nonstandard Measuring Tool

COMMON CORE STANDARD—1.MD.2
Measure lengths indirectly and by iterating length units.

Use the measuring tool you made. Measure real objects.

1.

about _____ 🖇

2.

about _____ 🖇

3.

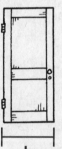

about _____ 🖇

4.

about _____ 🖇

5.

about _____ 🖇

6.

about _____ 🖇

7.

about _____ 🖇

8.

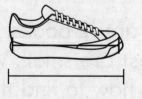

about _____ 🖇

Lesson Check (1.MD.2)

1. Use the ⊂⊃ below. Circle the
   string that is about 4 ⊂⊃ long.

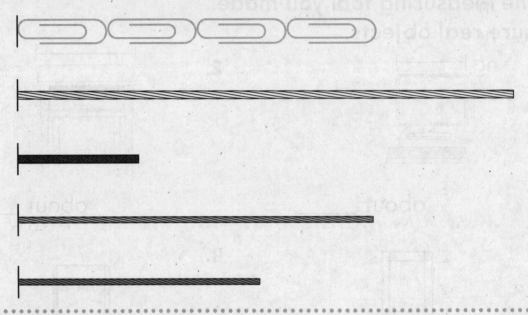

· ·

Spiral Review (1.OA.1, 1.NBT.3)

2. Ty crosses out the number cards
   that are greater than 38 and less
   than 34. What numbers are left?

   33   35   37   39   40

   _____ and _____

· ·

3. There are 12 books. 4 books are large.
   The rest are small. Write a number sentence that
   shows how to find the number of small books.

   _____ − _____ = _____

Problem Solving • Measure and Compare

COMMON CORE STANDARD—1.MD.2
Measure lengths indirectly and by iterating length units.

The blue string is about 3 ⚬ long. The green string is 2 ⚬ longer than the blue string. The red string is 1 ⚬ shorter than the blue string. Measure and draw the strings in order from **longest** to **shortest**.

1. |

   about ____ ⚬

2. |

   about ____ ⚬

3. |

   about ____ ⚬

Problem Solving *Real World*

4. Sandy has a ribbon about 4 ⚬ long. She cut a new ribbon 2 ⚬ longer. Measure and draw the two ribbons.

   |

   |

   The new ribbon is about ____ ⚬ long.

Lesson Check (1.MD.2)

1. Mia measures a stapler with her paper clip ruler. About how long is the stapler?

about _____ ⌗

Spiral Review (1.OA.6, 1.NBT.1)

2. What is the unknown number? Write the number.

$$4 + \underline{\quad} = 13$$

3. Count by tens. What numbers are missing? Write the numbers.

17, 27, _____, _____, 57, 67

Time to the Hour

COMMON CORE STANDARD—1.MD.3
Tell and write time.

**Look at where the hour hand points.
Write the time.**

1.

_____

2.

_____

3.

_____

4.

_____

5.

_____

6.

_____

Problem Solving Real World

Solve.

7. Which time is **not** the same? Circle it.

7:00   7 o'clock

Lesson Check (1.MD.3)

I. Look at the hour hand. What is the time? Write the time.

_____

2. Look at the hour hand. What is the time? Write the time.

____ o'clock

Spiral Review (1.NBT.4)

3. What is the sum? Write the number.

$$40 + 30 = \underline{\qquad}$$

4. What is the sum? Write the number.

$$53 + 30 = \underline{\qquad}$$

Name _____

Time to the Half Hour

COMMON CORE STANDARD—1.MD.3
Tell and write time.

Look at where the hour hand points.
Write the time.

1.

_____

- - - - - - - -

_____

2.

_____

- - - - - - - -

_____

3.

_____

- - - - - - - -

_____

4.

_____

- - - - - - - -

_____

5.

_____

- - - - - - - -

_____

6.

_____

- - - - - - - -

_____

Problem Solving Real World

Solve.

7. Greg rides his bike at half past 4:00. He eats dinner at half past 6:00. He reads a book at half past 8:00.

Look at the clock.
Write what Greg does.

Greg _____

- - - - - - - - - - - -

_____.

Lesson Check (1.MD.3)

1. Look at the hour hand. What is the time?
   Write the time.

_____

2. Look at the hour hand. What is the time?
   Write the time.

_____

Spiral Review (1.NBT.1, 1.NBT.2b)

3. What number does the model show?
   Write the number.

_____

4. How many tens and ones make this number?

14
fourteen

_____ ten _____ ones

© Houghton Mifflin Harcourt Publishing Company

Tell Time to the Hour and Half Hour

COMMON CORE STANDARD—1.MD.3
Tell and write time.

Write the time.

1.

2.

3.

4.

5.

6.

Problem Solving Real World

Solve.

7. Lulu walks her dog at 7 o'clock. Bill walks his dog 30 minutes later. Draw to show what time Bill walks his dog.

Lesson Check (1.MD.3)

1. What time is it?
   Write the time.

_____

2. What time is it?
   Write the time.

_____

Spiral Review (1.NBT.4)

3. What is the sum?
   Write the number.

   $48 + 20 =$ ___

4. How many tens and ones
   are in the sum? Write the
   numbers. Write the sum.

   $$\begin{array}{r} 67 \\ + 25 \\ \hline \end{array}$$

   ___ tens ___ ones

Name _____

Practice Time to the Hour and Half Hour

COMMON CORE STANDARD—1.MD.3
Tell and write time.

Use the hour hand to write the time. Draw the minute hand.

1.

2.

3.

4.

5.

6.

Problem Solving Real World

Solve.

7. Billy played outside for a half hour. Write how many minutes Billy played outside.

_____ minutes

Lesson Check (1.MD.3)

1. Write the time.

_____

Spiral Review (1.NBT.6, 1.MD.2)

2. What is the difference?
Write the number.

$$80 - 30 = \underline{\quad}$$

3. Use ■. Amy measures the eraser with ■.
About how long is the eraser?

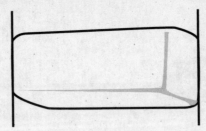

about _____ ■ long

P176 one hundred seventy-six

School-Home Letter

Dear Family,

My class started Chapter 10 this week. In this chapter, I will show data with tally charts and graphs. I will also ask and answer questions about the charts and graphs.

Love, _____

Vocabulary

bar graph a graph that uses bars to show information

picture graph a graph that uses pictures to show information

tally chart a chart that uses tally marks to record information

tally mark a line that stands for one person or thing

Home Activity

Help your child keep track of the weather on a calendar for a week or longer. Then help your child use the data to make a picture graph. Use the graph to compare the number of days that were sunny, cloudy, and rainy.

Weather This Week							
sunny	○	○	○	○			
cloudy	○	○	○				
rainy	○						

Each ○ stands for 1 day.

Literature

Look for these books in a library. These books will reinforce your child's understanding of data and graphs.

The Great Graph Contest by Loreen Leedy. Holiday House, 2006.

Graphing Favorite Things by Jennifer Marrewa. Weekly Reader® Books, 2008.

Carta para la casa

Querida familia:

Mi clase comenzó el Capítulo 10 esta semana. En este capítulo, mostraré datos con tablas de conteo y gráficas. También haré y responderé preguntas sobre tablas y gráficas.

Con cariño, _____

Vocabulario

gráfica de barras una gráfica que utiliza barras para mostrar información

pictografía una gráfica que utiliza dibujos para mostrar información

tabla de conteo una tabla que utiliza marcas para registrar información

marca de conteo una línea que representa una persona o una cosa

Actividad para la casa

Ayude a su hijo para que siga el clima usando un calendario durante una semana o más. Luego ayude a su hijo para que use los datos para hacer una pictografía. Usen la gráfica para comparar el número de días soleados, nublados y lluviosos.

Las condiciones del tiempo durante esta semana							
soleado	○	○	○	○			
nublado	○	○	○				
lluvioso	○						

Cada ○ representa I diá.

Literatura

Busque estos libros en una biblioteca. Estos libros reforzarán el aprendizaje de su hijo sobre datos y gráficas.

The Great Graph Contest por Loreen Leedy. Holiday House, 2006.

Graphing Favorite Things por Jennifer Marrewa. Weekly Reader® Books, 2008. Albert Whitman and Company, 1993.

Name _____

Read Picture Graphs

COMMON CORE STANDARD—1.MD.4
Represent and interpret data.

Our Favorite Outdoor Activity

🚲 biking	🧍	🧍	🧍	🧍	🧍	🧍	🧍	🧍
🛹 skating	🧍	🧍						
🏃 running	🧍	🧍	🧍	🧍				

Each 🧍 stands for 1 child.

Use the picture graph to answer the question.

1. How many children chose 🚲?

_____ children

2. How many children chose 🛹 and 🏃 altogether?

_____ children

3. Which activity did the most children choose? Circle.

Problem Solving Real World

Write a number sentence to solve the problem.
Use the picture graph at the top of the page.

4. How many more children chose 🚲 than 🏃?

_____ more children

Lesson Check (1.MD.4)

Use the picture graph to answer the question.

Do you do chores at home?								
yes	☺	☺	☺	☺	☺	☺	☺	☺
no	☺	☺	☺	☺	☺	☺		

Each ☺ stands for I child.

1. How many children do chores at home?
   Write the number.

   _____ children

2. How many more children answered yes
   than no? Write a number sentence to
   solve the problem.

   _____ more children   ___○___○___

Spiral Review (1.NBT.1, 1.NBT.5)

3. What number is ten less than 82?
   Circle the number. Then write the
   number sentence.

   92   83   81   72

   _____ − 10 = _____

4. Count forward. What number is missing?
   Write the number.

   110, 111, 112, _____, 114

Name _____

Make Picture Graphs

COMMON CORE STANDARD—1.MD.4
Represent and interpret data.

Which dinosaur do the most children like best? Ask 10 friends.
Draw 1 circle for each child's answer.

Our Favorite Dinosaur										
🦖 Tyrannosaurus										
🦕 Triceratops										
🦕 Apatosaurus										

Each ○ stands for 1 child.

Use the picture graph to answer the question.

1. How many children chose ?

   _____ children

2. How many children chose and altogether?

   _____ children

3. Which dinosaur did the fewest children choose? Circle.

4. Which dinosaur did the most children choose? Circle.

Problem Solving Real World

5. Write your own question about the graph.

   _____

   _____

   _____

   _____

Lesson Check (1.MD.4)

Use the picture graph to answer the question.

Which Hand Do You Use to Eat?								
left	○	○	○					
right	○	○	○	○	○	○	○	○

Each ○ stands for 1 child.

1. How many children use their right hand?
   Write the answer.

   ____ children

2. How many more children use their right
   hand than their left? Write a number
   sentence to solve the problem.

   ____ more children   ____ ○ ____ ○ ____

Spiral Review (1.OA.6 , 1.NBT.6)

3. Write is the sum.

   $$6 + 3 = \underline{}$$

4. Write the difference. Write how many tens.

   $$60 - 20 = \underline{}$$

   ____ tens

Name _____

Read Bar Graphs

COMMON CORE STANDARD—1.MD.4
Represent and interpret data.

Use the bar graph to answer the question.

1. How many children chose ◯?

   _____ children

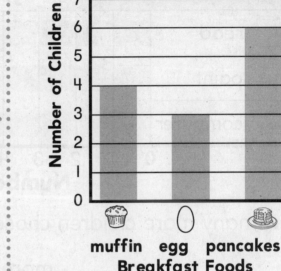

2. How many children chose 🧁?

   _____ children

3. How many children chose 🧁 or ◯?

   _____ children

4. How many more children chose 🥞 than ◯?

   _____ more children

Problem Solving *Real World*

Use the bar graph to answer the question.

5. Claudette uses an ☂. Add her to the graph. Now how many more children use an ☂ than a 🎩?

   _____ more children

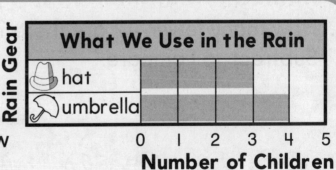

Lesson Check (1.MD.4)

Use the bar graph to answer the question.

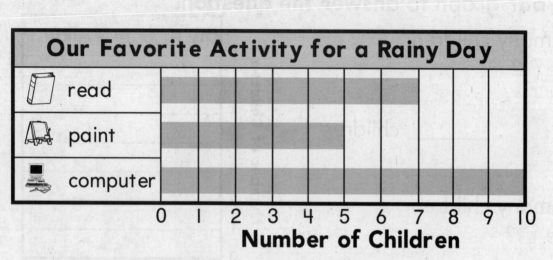

1. How many more children chose 🖥 than 🎨?

_____ more children

Spiral Review (1.OA.4, 1.OA.8)

2. Write a subtraction sentence you can solve by using $9 + 7 = 16$.

___ − ___ = ___

3. How many fewer ⚾ are there?
Subtract to compare.

$7 - 5 =$ ___

___ fewer

Make Bar Graphs

COMMON CORE STANDARD—1.MD.4
Represent and interpret data.

Which is your favorite meal?

1. Ask 10 friends which meal they like best.
Make a bar graph.

Our Favorite Meal

Meal											
breakfast											
lunch											
dinner											

0 1 2 3 4 5 6 7 8 9 10
Number of Children

2. How many children chose breakfast?

_____ children

3. Which meal was chosen by the most children?

_____

Problem Solving

4. What if 10 children chose breakfast?
How many children could choose lunch or dinner?

_____ children

Lesson Check (1.MD.4)

Use the bar graph to answer the question.

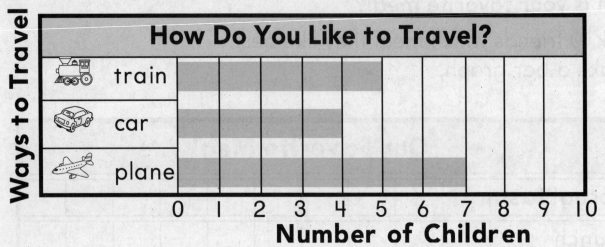

1. How many more children chose ✈ than 🚂?

   _____ more children

Spiral Review (1.OA.6, 1.NBT.4)

2. Write the number sentence that completes the related facts.

$$7 + 8 = 15 \qquad 15 - 8 = 7$$
$$8 + 7 = 15$$

$$\boxed{} - \boxed{} = \boxed{}$$

3. What is the sum? Use tens and ones to add.

$$\begin{array}{r} 43 \\ + 21 \\ \hline \end{array}$$

   4 tens + 3 ones
   2 tens + 1 one
   _____

   ____ tens + ____ ones

   ____ + ____ = ____

Name _____

Read Tally Charts

COMMON CORE STANDARD—1.MD.4
Represent and interpret data.

Complete the tally chart.

Our Favorite Vegetable		Total
beans	IIII	
corn	IIII III	
carrots	IIII	

Use the tally chart to answer each question.

1. How many children chose ? _____ children

2. How many children chose ? _____ children

3. How many more children chose than ? _____ more children

4. Which vegetable did the most children choose? Circle.

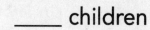

Problem Solving Real World

Complete each sentence about the tally chart.
Write **greater than**, **less than**, or **equal to**.

5. The number of children who chose ⌒ is
_____ the number who chose 🥕 .

6. The number of children who chose 🌽 is
_____ the number who chose ⌒ .

Lesson Check (1.MD.4)

Use the tally chart to answer each question.

Our Favorite Pet		
🐕	dog	卌 ‖
🐈	cat	卌
🐟	fish	‖

1. How many children chose ?

   _____ children

2. How many more children chose than ?

   _____ more children

Spiral Review (1.OA.1, 1.NBT.4)

3. Complete the number sentence.

   There are 8 apples.
   6 apples are red.
   The rest are green.
   How many apples are green?

   $\underline{\quad 8 \quad} \ominus \underline{\quad 6 \quad} \ominus \underline{\qquad}$

4. Write the sum.

   $34 + 40 = \underline{\qquad}$

© Houghton Mifflin Harcourt Publishing Company

Make Tally Charts

HANDS ON
Lesson 10.6

COMMON CORE STANDARD—1.MD.4
Represent and interpret data.

Which color do most children like best? Ask 10 friends. Make 1 tally mark for each child's answer.

Favorite Color		Total
red		
blue		

1. How many children chose red?

_____ **children**

2. How many children chose blue?

_____ **children**

3. Circle the color that was chosen by fewer children.

red   blue

Problem Solving Real World

Jason asked 10 friends to choose their favorite game. He will ask 10 more children.

Our Favorite Game	
tag	I
kickball	卌 II
hopscotch	II

4. Predict. Which game will children most likely choose?

_____

5. Predict. Which game will children least likely choose?

_____

Lesson Check (1.MD.4)

1. Which insect did the most children choose?
   Circle the answer.

Our Favorite Insect		Total
ladybug	III	3
bee	I	1
butterfly	⊮ II	7

Spiral Review (1.NBT.2b, 1.NBT.3)

2. Circle the number that is greater than 54.
   Write the numbers.

   45   50   54   57

   _____ is greater than 54.

   _____ > 54

3. Use the model. Write the number
   three different ways.

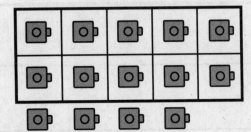

   _____ ten _____ ones

   _____ + _____

Problem Solving • Represent Data

COMMON CORE STANDARD—1.MD.4
Represent and interpret data.

Bella made a tally chart to show the favorite sport of 10 friends.

Our Favorite Sport	
Soccer	卌 I
Basketball	III
Baseball	I

Use the tally chart to make a bar graph.

Our Favorite Sport

Kinds of Sports

Soccer								
Basketball								
Baseball								

0 1 2 3 4 5 6 7 8

Number of Children

Use the graph to solve.

1. How many friends chose soccer?

_____ friends

2. How many friends chose soccer or basketball?

_____ friends

Lesson Check (1.MD.4)

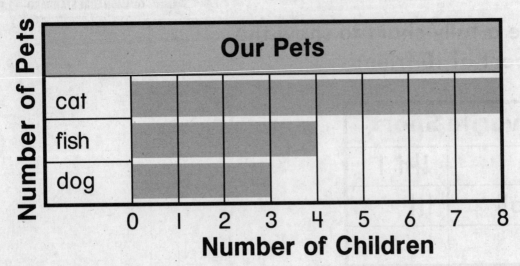

Our Pets

Number of Pets: cat, fish, dog

Number of Children: 0 1 2 3 4 5 6 7 8

1. Use the graph. How many more children have fish than a dog?

_____ more

Spiral Review (1.MD.1, 1.MD.3)

2. Which ribbon is the shortest? Color the shortest ribbon.

3. Look at the hour hand. Write the time.

_____

School-Home Letter

Dear Family,

My class started Chapter 11 this week. In this chapter, I will learn about three-dimensional shapes. I will learn how to make objects and larger shapes from other shapes.

Love, _____

Vocabulary

flat surface

curved surface

Home Activity

Use a paper towel roll (cylinder), a tennis ball (sphere), a cube-shaped box or building block (cube), and a book (rectangular prism). Build objects using these or other household items of the same shapes. Have children name each shape used in the objects you make.

Literature

Look for these books in a library. Point out shapes and how they can be found in everyday objects.

The Greedy Triangle
Marilyn Burns.
Scholastic, 2008.

Captain Invincible and the Space Shapes
Stuart J. Murphy.
HarperCollins Publishers, 2001.

Carta para la casa

Querida familia:

Mi clase comenzó el Capítulo 11 esta semana. En este capítulo, aprenderé sobre las guras tridimensionales. Aprenderé a hacer objetos y guras más grandes tomando como base otras guras.

Con cariño, _____

Vocabulario

superficie plana

superficie curva

Actividad para la casa

Use un rollo de papel (cilindro), una pelota de tenis (esfera), una caja con forma de cubo o un bloque de construcción (cubo) y un libro (prisma rectangular). Construya objetos usando estas u otras cosas con formas similares que encuentre en la casa. Pídale a su hijo que nombre cada figura usada en los objetos que usted haga.

Literatura

Busque estos libros en una biblioteca. Señale las figuras y muestre a su hijo cómo las puede encontrar en los objetos que ve a diario.

The Greedy Triangle
por Marilyn Burns.
Scholastic, 2008.

Captain Invincible and the Space Shapes
por Stuart J. Murphy.
HarperCollins
Publishers, 2001.

Name _____

Three-Dimensional Shapes

COMMON CORE STANDARD—1.G.1
Reason with shapes and their attributes.

**Use three-dimensional shapes.
Write the number of flat surfaces
for each shape.**

1. A cylinder has __ flat surfaces.

....

2. A rectangular prism has __ flat surfaces.

....

3. A cone has __ flat surface.

....

4. A cube has __ flat surfaces.

....

Problem Solving Real World

5. Circle the object that matches the clue.
Mike finds an object that has only a curved surface.

Lesson Check (1.G.1)

1. Circle the shape that has both flat and curved surfaces.

 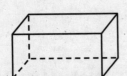

2. Circle the shape that has only a curved surface.

Spiral Review (1.OA.1, 1.NBT.1)

3. Count forward. Write the number that is missing.

$$109, \ 110, \ 111, \ \underline{\quad}, \ 113$$

4. What is the sum of 2 and 3? Write the number sentence.

Name _____

Combine Three-Dimensional Shapes

COMMON CORE STANDARD—1.G.2
Reason with shapes and their attributes.

Use three-dimensional shapes.

Combine.	Which new shape can you make? Circle it.
1. 	
2.	
3.	

Problem Solving Real World

4. Circle the shapes you could use to model the bird feeder.

Lesson Check (1.G.2)

I. Circle the shape that combines ▢ and △.

Spiral Review (1.OA.1, 1.NBT.4)

2. Write the sum. Write how many tens.

$40 + 20 =$ ___   ___ tens

3. Emi has 15 crayons.
She gives some crayons to Jo.
Now she has 9 crayons.
How many crayons did
Emi give to Jo?
Use the model to solve.

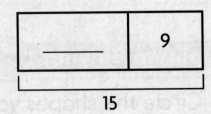

___ crayons

Name _____

Make New Three-Dimensional Shapes

COMMON CORE STANDARD—1.G.2
Reason with shapes and their attributes.

Use three-dimensional shapes.

Build and Repeat.

Combine. Which new shape can you make? Circle it.

1.

2.

3.

Problem Solving Real World

4. Dave builds this shape.
   Then he repeats and combines.
   Draw a shape he can make.

Lesson Check (1.G.2)

1. Which new shape can you make? Circle the shape.

Combine 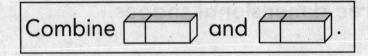 and .

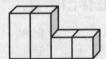

Spiral Review (1.OA.4, 1.OA.6)

2. Which addition fact helps you solve $15 - 6 = $ ___?
Write the number sentence.

$$\underline{\quad} + \underline{\quad} = \underline{\quad}$$

3. Which doubles fact helps you solve $5 + 6 = 11$?
Circle the number sentence.

$3 + 3 = 6$ $4 + 4 = 8$

$5 + 5 = 10$ $7 + 7 = 14$

Name _____

Problem Solving • Take Apart Three-Dimensional Shapes

COMMON CORE STANDARD—1.G.2
Reason with shapes and their attributes.

**Use three-dimensional shapes.
Circle your answer.**

1. Paco used shapes to build this robot. Circle the shapes he used.

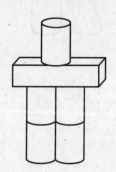

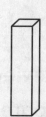

2. Eva used shapes to build this wall. Circle the shapes she used.

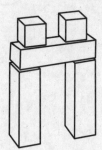

Problem Solving Real World

3. Circle the ways that show the same shape.

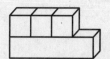

Lesson Check (1.G.2)

1. Lara made this picture frame.
   Circle the shapes she
   used to make the frame.

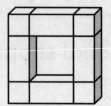

Spiral Review (1.NBT.3, 1.NBT.4, 1.NBT.6)

2. Compare each pair of numbers.
   Write <, >, or =.

   13 $\bigcirc$ 31   13 $\bigcirc$ 13   31 $\bigcirc$ 13   31 $\bigcirc$ 31

3. Subtract. What is the difference?
   Write the number.

$$60 - 30 = \underline{\qquad}$$

Name _____

Two-Dimensional Shapes on Three-Dimensional Shapes

COMMON CORE STANDARD—1.G.1
Reason with shapes and their attributes.

Circle the objects you could trace to draw the shape.

1.

2.

3.

Problem Solving *Real World*

4. Look at this shape. Draw the shape you would make if you traced this object.

Lesson Check

1. Which flat surface does a cone have?
Circle the shape.

2. Which flat surfaces could a rectangular prism have?
Circle the pair of shapes.

  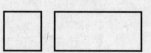

Spiral Review (1.OA.3, 1.OA.5)

Write a subtraction sentence to solve.

3. Jade has 8 books.
She gives some of them to Dana.
Now Jade has 6 books.
How many did she give to Dana?

_____ − _____ = _____

_____ books

4. Write the sum.

$$3 + 0 = \underline{\qquad}$$

P204 two hundred four

© Houghton Mifflin Harcourt Publishing Company

School-Home Letter

Dear Family,

My class started Chapter 12 this week. In this chapter, I will describe and combine two-dimensional shapes. I will learn about equal shares, halves, and fourths.

Love, _____

Vocabulary

hexagon

trapezoid

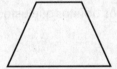

Home Activity

Use a napkin (square), a folded napkin (triangle), and an envelope (rectangle). Combine these items or other household items of the same shapes to make new shapes. Have your child name each shape used in the new shapes you made.

Literature

Look for these books in a library. Point out shapes and how they can be found in everyday objects.

The Greedy Triangle by Marilyn Burns. Scholastic, 2008.

Color Farm by Lois Ehlert. HarperCollins, 1990.

Carta
para la casa

Querida familia:

Mi clase comenzó el Capítulo 12 esta semana. En este capítulo, aprenderé sobre guras bidimensionales. Aprenderé cómo hacer guras más grandes que otras.

Con cariño, _____

Vocabulario

hexágono

trapecio

Actividad para la casa

Use una servilleta (cuadrado), una servilleta doblada (triángulo) y un sobre (rectángulo). Construya objetos usando estos u otros elementos de la casa con las mismas formas. Pídales a los niños que nombren cada figura usada en los objetos que usted hace.

Literatura

Busque estos libros en una biblioteca. Señale las figuras y muestre cómo se pueden encontrar en los objetos de la vida diaria.

The Greedy Triangle por Marilyn Burns. Scholastic, 2008.

Color Farm by Lois Ehlert. HarperCollins, 1990.

Name _____

Sort Two-Dimensional Shapes

COMMON CORE STANDARD—1.G.1
Reason with shapes and their attributes.

Read the sorting rule. Circle the shapes that follow the rule.

1. **not** curved

2. 4 vertices

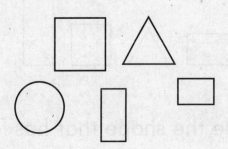

3. more than 3 sides

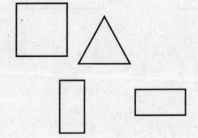

4. curved

Problem Solving *Real World*

5. Katie sorted these shapes.
   Write a sorting rule
   to tell how Katie sorted.

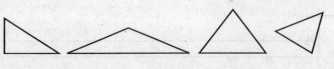

_____

_ _ _ _ _ _ _ _ _ _ _ _ _ _ _ _ _

Lesson Check (1.G.1)

1. Circle the shape that would **not** be sorted into this group.

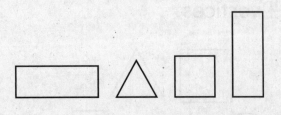   

2. Circle the shape that has fewer than 4 sides.

Spiral Review (1.MD.1)

Solve. Draw or write to explain.

3. Clue 1: A black line is shorter than a white line.
Clue 2: The white line is shorter than a gray line.
Is the black line longer or shorter
than the gray line? _____
_ _ _ _ _ _ _ _ _ _ _ _ _ _ _ _ _
_____

Name _____

Describe Two-Dimensional Shapes

COMMON CORE STANDARD—1.G.1
Reason with shapes and their attributes.

Use [BLUE] to trace each straight side. Use [RED] to circle each vertex. Write the number of sides and vertices.

I.
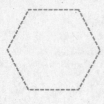
_____ sides

_____ vertices

2.
_____ sides

_____ vertices

3.
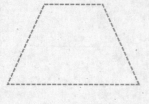
_____ sides

_____ vertices

4.

_____ sides

_____ vertices

5.
_____ sides

_____ vertices

6.

_____ sides

_____ vertices

Problem Solving

Draw a shape to match the clues.

7. Ying draws a shape with 4 sides. She labels it as a rectangle.

Lesson Check (1.G.1)

1. How many vertices does a triangle have?

_____ vertices

2. How many vertices does a ☐ have?

_____ vertices

Spiral Review (1.OA.5, 1.MD.2)

3. Circle the greater addend.
Count on to find the sum.

$$\begin{array}{r} 2 \\ + 9 \\ \hline \end{array}$$

4. Corey measures a crayon box with his paper clip ruler. About how long is the box?

about _____ ⊂⊃

Combine Two-Dimensional Shapes

COMMON CORE STANDARD—1.G.2
Reason with shapes and their attributes.

Use pattern blocks. Draw to show the blocks. Write how many blocks you used.

1. How many △ make a ⬠ ?

_____ △ make a ⬠ .

2. How many △ make a ◇ ?

_____ △ make a ◇ .

Problem Solving Real World

Use pattern blocks. Draw to show your answer.

3. 2 ⬠ make a ⬡ .

How many ⬠ make 4 ⬡ ?

_____ ⬠ make 4 ⬡ .

Lesson Check (1.G.2)

1. How many △ do you use to make a ⬡?

____ △ make a ⬡.

2. How many ◇ do you use to make a ⬡?

____ ◇ make a ⬡.

Spiral Review (1.MD.2, 1.MD.3)

3. Use ⌷. Which string is about 5 ⌷ long?
   Circle the string that is about 5 ⌷ long.

4. Look at the hour hand. Write the time.

____

Combine More Shapes

COMMON CORE STANDARD—1.G.2
Reason with shapes and their attributes.

Circle two shapes that can combine to make the shape on the left.

1.

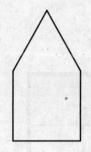 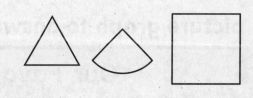

2.

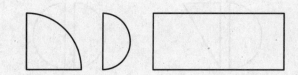

3.

Problem Solving Real World

4. Draw lines to show how the shapes on the left combine to make the new shape.

   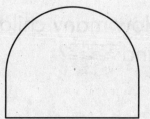

Lesson Check (1.G.2)

1. Circle the shapes that can combine to make this new shape.

. . . .

Spiral Review (1.MD.4)

Use the picture graph to answer each question.

Our Favorite Activity						
🏊 Swimming	👤	👤	👤			
🩰 Dancing	👤	👤	👤	👤		
🖍 Drawing	👤	👤	👤	👤	👤	👤

Each 👤 stands for 1 child.

2. How many more children chose 🖍 than 🏊?

_____ more children

. . . .

3. How many children chose 🩰 and 🏊?

_____ children

Problem Solving • Make New Two-Dimensional Shapes

COMMON CORE STANDARD—1.G.2
Reason with shapes and their attributes.

Use shapes to solve.
Draw to show your work.

1. Use ▢ to make a ▭.
   Step 1. Combine shapes to make a new shape.

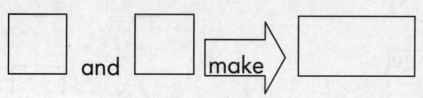

Step 2. Then use the new shape.

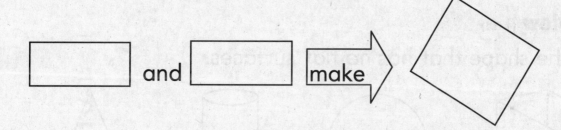

2. Use ◺ to make a ◯.
   Step 1. Combine shapes to make a new shape.

Step 2. Then use the new shape.

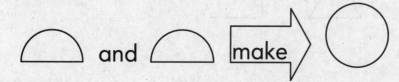

Lesson Check (1.G.2)

Follow the steps.

1. Which new shape could you make?
   Circle your answer.

Step 1.
Combine 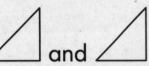 and to make .

Step 2.
Then use 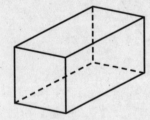 and 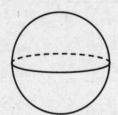.

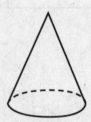

Spiral Review (1.G.1)

2. Circle the shape that has no flat surfaces.

3. Which flat surface does a cylinder have?
   Circle your answer.

© Houghton Mifflin Harcourt Publishing Company

P216 two hundred sixteen

Name _____

Find Shapes in Shapes

COMMON CORE STANDARD—1.G.2
Reason with shapes and their attributes.

Use two pattern blocks to make the shape. Draw a line to show your model. Circle the blocks you use.

1.

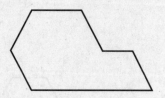

2.

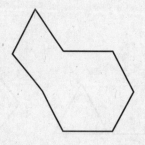

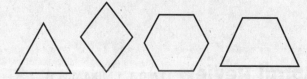

3.

4.

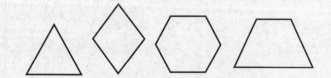

Problem Solving Real World

Make the shape to the right. Use the number of pattern blocks listed in the exercise. Write how many of each block you use.

5. Use 3 blocks.

Lesson Check (1.G.2)

1. Circle the pair of pattern blocks that can make this shape.

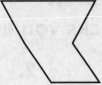

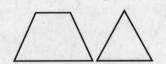 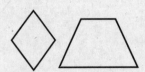 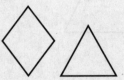 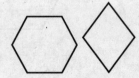

Spiral Review (1.MD.3, 1.MD.4, 1.G.1)

2. Write the time.

_____

---

3. Write tally marks to show the number 8.

_____

---

4. How many vertices does a ☐ have?

_____ vertices

Name _____

Take Apart Two-Dimensional Shapes

COMMON CORE STANDARD—1.G.2
Reason with shapes and their attributes.

Draw a line to show the parts.

1. Show 2 .

2. Show 2 .

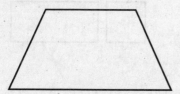

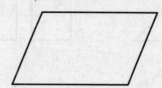

3. Show 1 and 1 .

4. Show 1 and 1 .

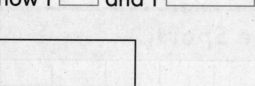

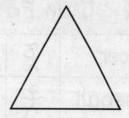

Problem Solving Real World

5. How many triangles are there?

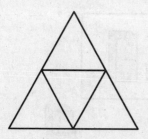

_____ triangles

Lesson Check (1.G.2)

1. Look at the picture. Circle the pair that shows the parts.

   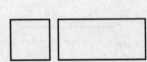

- -

Spiral Review (1.MD.4, 1.G.2)

2. Use the graph. How many children chose ⚽ ?

Our Favorite Sport								
⚽ soccer	人	人						
⚾ baseball	人	人	人	人	人	人		
🎾 tennis	人	人	人	人	人			

Each 人 stands for 1 child.

_____ children

- -

3. Which new shape can you make? Circle your answer.

Combine  and .

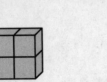 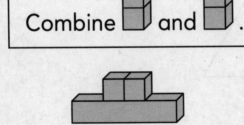

Equal or Unequal Parts

COMMON CORE STANDARD—1.G.3
Reason with shapes and their attributes.

Color the shapes that show unequal shares.

1.

 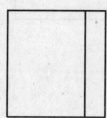 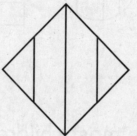 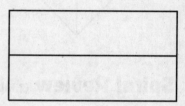

Color the shapes that show equal shares.

2.

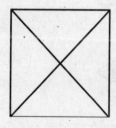 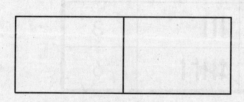 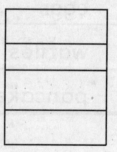 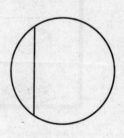

Problem Solving Real World

Draw lines to show the parts.

3. 4 equal shares

Lesson Check (1.G.3)

1. Color the shape that shows unequal shares.

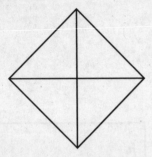 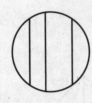 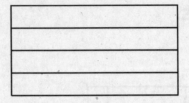

Spiral Review (1.MD.4)

2. Which food did the most children choose?
   Circle your answer.

Our Favorite Breakfast		Total
🍳 eggs	‖‖	4
🧇 waffles	‖‖	3
🥞 pancakes	‖‖‖‖	6

3. Use the graph. How many children chose 🧸?

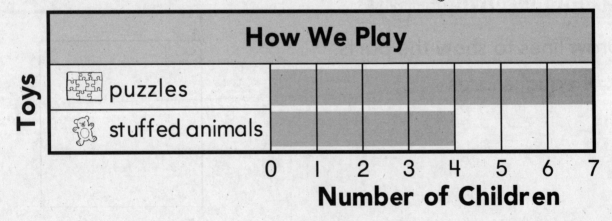

_____ children

Halves

COMMON CORE STANDARD—1.G.3
Reason with shapes and their attributes.

Circle the shapes that show halves.

1.

2.

3.

4.

5.

6.

7.

8.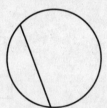

9.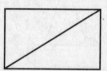

Problem Solving Real World

Draw or write to solve.

10. Kate cut a square into equal shares. She traced one of the parts. Write **half of** or **halves** to name the part.

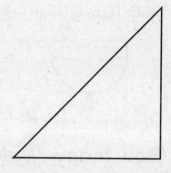

_____
_____ a square
_____

Lesson Check (1.G.3)

1. Circle the shape that shows halves.

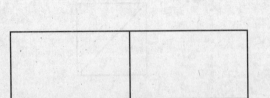 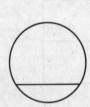 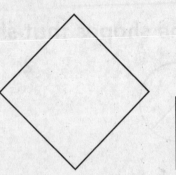

. . . .

Spiral Review (1.G.1, 1.G.2)

2. Circle the new shape you can make.

Combine ⬧ and ▣.

3. Circle the shape that has both
flat and curved surfaces.

4. How many △ do you use to make a ▱?
Draw to show your answer.

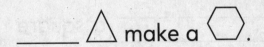

_____ △ make a ⬡.

Fourths

COMMON CORE STANDARD—1.G.3
Reason with shapes and their attributes.

Circle the shapes that show fourths.

1.

2.

3.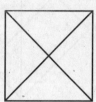

4.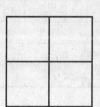

5.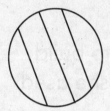

6.

7.

8.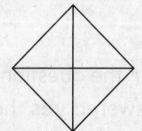

9.

Problem Solving *Real World*

Solve.

10. Chad drew a picture to show a quarter of a circle. Which shape did Chad draw? Circle it.

Lesson Check (1.G.3)

1. Circle the shape that shows fourths.

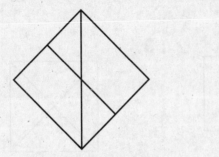 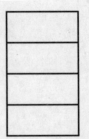 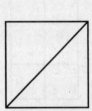

Spiral Review (1.MD.4, 1.G.2)

2. What shapes did Leila use to build the wall? Circle the shapes she used.

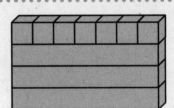

3. Use the graph to answer the question. How many fewer children answered **yes** than **no**?

Answer	Do You Have a Pet?						
yes	○	○	○	○			
no	○	○	○	○	○	○	

Number of Children

_____ fewer children

Algebra • Ways to Expand Numbers

Essential Question How can you write a two-digit number in different ways?

Model and Draw

There are different ways to think about a number.

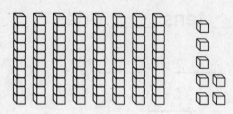

___8___ tens ___7___ ones

___80___ + ___7___

___87___

8 tens and 7 ones is the same as 80 plus 7.

Share and Show

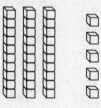

Write how many tens and ones.
Write the number in two different ways.

1.

____ tens ____ ones

____ + ____

____

2.

____ tens ____ ones

____ + ____

____

Math Talk Does the 7 in this number show 7 or 70? Explain.

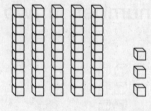

On Your Own

Write how many tens and ones.
Write the number in two different ways.

3.

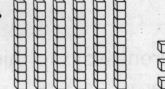

_____ tens _____ ones

_____ + _____

_____

4.

_____ tens _____ ones

_____ + _____

_____

Problem Solving · Real World

5. Draw the same number using only tens.
Write how many tens and ones.
Write the number in two different ways.

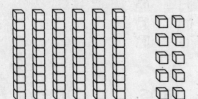

_____ tens _____ ones

_____ + _____

_____

_____ tens _____ ones

_____ + _____

_____

TAKE HOME ACTIVITY • Write a two-digit number to 99.
Ask your child to write how many tens and ones and then write the
number a different way.

P228 two hundred twenty-eight

© Houghton Mifflin Harcourt Publishing Company

Identify Place Value

Essential Question How can you use place value to understand the value of a number?

Model and Draw

The **1** in **1**25 means 1 hundred.
The **2** in 1**2**5 means 2 tens.
The **5** in 12**5** means 5 ones.

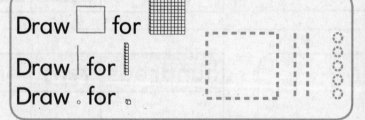

125

Draw ☐ for ▦
Draw | for |
Draw ₀ for ▫

hundreds	tens	ones
1	2	5

Share and Show

Use your MathBoard and to show the number.
Draw to complete the quick picture. Write how many hundreds, tens, and ones.

THINK
106 has no tens.

1.

106

hundreds	tens	ones
___	___	___

Math Talk   How is the 1 in 187 different from the 1 in 781?

On Your Own

Use your MathBoard and [blocks].
Draw to complete the quick picture.
Write how many hundreds, tens, and ones.

2.
170

hundreds	tens	ones
___	___	___

3.
143

hundreds	tens	ones
___	___	___

4.
121

hundreds	tens	ones
___	___	___

Problem Solving · Real World

Circle your answer.

5. I have 1 hundred, 9 tens, and 9 ones. What number am I?

99   100   199

6. I have 3 ones, 0 tens, and 1 hundred. What number am I?

107   170   103

TAKE HOME ACTIVITY • Write some numbers from 100 to 199. Have your child tell how many hundreds, tens, and ones are in the number.

Name _____

Use Place Value to Compare Numbers

Essential Question How can you use place value to compare two numbers?

I want to eat the greater number.

Model and Draw

Use these symbols to compare numbers.

> is greater than
< is less than
= is equal to

45 **46**

$45 < 46$
45 is less than 46.

Compare 134 and 125.

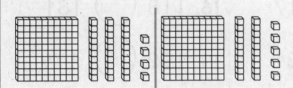

First compare hundreds.
One hundred is equal to one hundred.
$100 = 100$
If the hundreds are equal, compare the tens. 30 is greater than 20.
$134 > 125$

Share and Show

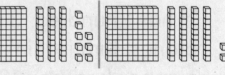

Write the numbers and compare. Write >, <, or =.

1.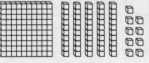

$\underline{159} \;\bigodot\; \underline{155}$

2.

$\underline{} \;\bigcirc\; \underline{}$

Compare the numbers using >, <, or =.

3. 187 $\bigcirc$ 168

4. 165 $\bigcirc$ 159

5. 127 $\bigcirc$ 141

 Math Talk Compare 173 and 177. Did you have to compare all the digits? Why or why not?

Getting Ready for Grade 2

two hundred thirty-one **P231**

Write the numbers. Compare. Write $>$, $<$, or $=$.

6. 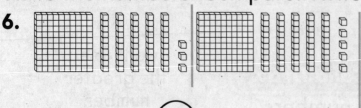 7.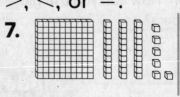

___ ◯ ___   ___ ◯ ___

Compare the numbers using $>$, $<$, or $=$.

8. 143 ◯ 143   9. 162 ◯ 157   10. 185 ◯ 188

11. 124 ◯ 129   12. 189 ◯ 195   13. 135 ◯ 135

14. 173 ◯ 164   15. 123 ◯ 117   16. 118 ◯ 131

17. 155 ◯ 145   18. 181 ◯ 181   19. 192 ◯ 179

20. 122 ◯ 129   21. 166 ◯ 177   22. 154 ◯ 154

Problem Solving Real World

23. Antonio is thinking of a number between 100 and 199. It has 1 hundred, 3 tens, and 6 ones. Kim is thinking of a number between 100 and 199. It has 1 hundred, 6 tens, and 3 ones. Who is thinking of a greater number?

Draw or write to explain.

_____ is thinking of a greater number.

 TAKE HOME ACTIVITY • Choose two numbers between 100 and 199 and have your child explain which number is greater.

✓ Checkpoint

Concepts and Skills

Write how many tens and ones.
Write the number in two ways.

1.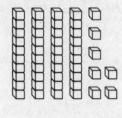

_____ tens and _____ ones

_____ + _____

_____

2.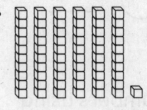

_____ tens and _____ one

_____ + _____

_____

Use your MathBoard and ▦▯.
Draw to complete the quick picture.
Write how many hundreds, tens, and ones.

3. 154

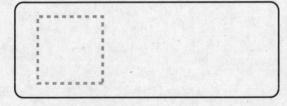

hundreds	tens	ones
_____	_____	_____

4. 128

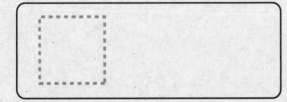

hundreds	tens	ones
_____	_____	_____

Write the numbers and compare. Write $>$, $<$, or $=$.

5.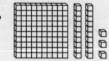

___ ◯ ___

6.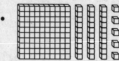

___ ◯ ___

Compare the numbers using $>$, $<$, or $=$.

7. 175 ◯ 175

9. 189 ◯ 188

11. 157 ◯ 157

8. 163 ◯ 173

10. 142 ◯ 158

12. 185 ◯ 180

13. Which comparison is correct?

○ 132 > 131

○ 131 = 132

○ 131 > 132

Name _____

Algebra • Addition Function Tables

Essential Question How can you follow a rule to complete an addition function table?

Model and Draw

The rule is Add 9. Add 9 to each number.

Add 9	
7	16
8	17
9	18

Share and Show

MATH BOARD

Follow a rule to complete the table.

1.
Add 3	
7	
8	
9	

2.
Add 4	
6	
7	
8	

3.
Add 5	
5	
7	
9	

4.
Add 8	
5	
7	
9	

5.
Add 7	
6	
8	
9	

6.
Add 6	
6	
8	
9	

Math Talk Look at Exercise 4. How does the rule help you see a pattern?

Getting Ready for Grade 2

Follow a rule to complete the table.

7.

Add 7	
7	
8	
9	

8.

Add 4	
7	
8	
9	

9.

Add 5	
7	
8	
9	

10.

Add 8	
4	
6	
8	
9	

11.

Add 3	
3	
5	
7	
9	

12.

Add 6	
6	
7	
8	
9	

Problem Solving

13. Solve. Complete the table.

Tom is 8 years old.
Julie is 7 years old.
Carla is 4 years old.

How old will each child
be in 4 years?

Tom	8	
Julie	7	
Carla	4	

TAKE HOME ACTIVITY • Copy Exercise 12 and change the numbers in the
left column to 9, 7, 5, and 3. Have your child complete the table and
explain how he or she used a rule to solve the problem.

Name _____

Algebra • Subtraction Function Tables

Essential Question How can you follow a rule to complete a subtraction function table?

Model and Draw

The rule is Subtract 7. Subtract 7 from each number.

Subtract 7	
14	7
15	8
16	9

Share and Show

Follow a rule to complete the table.

1.
Subtract 3	
9	
10	
11	

2.
Subtract 4	
6	
8	
10	

3.
Subtract 5	
6	
8	
10	

4.
Subtract 8	
9	
11	
13	

5.
Subtract 7	
12	
13	
14	

6.
Subtract 6	
6	
8	
9	

Math Talk How can Exercise 2 help you solve Exercise 3?

Follow a rule to complete the table.

7.
Subtract 4	
11	
12	
13	

8.
Subtract 6	
7	
8	
9	

9.
Subtract 5	
7	
8	
9	

10.
Subtract 7	
13	
14	
15	
16	

11.
Subtract 8	
12	
14	
16	
17	

12.
Subtract 9	
12	
14	
16	
17	

Problem Solving Real World

13. Solve. Complete the table.

Jane has 4 cookies.
Lucy has 3 cookies.
Seamus has 2 cookies.

How many cookies will each child have if they each eat 2 cookies?

Jane	4	
Lucy	3	
Seamus	2	

TAKE HOME ACTIVITY • Copy Exercise 12 and change the numbers in the left column to 10, 11, 12, and 13. Have your child complete the table and explain how he or she used a rule to solve the problem.

Name _____

Algebra • Follow the Rule

Essential Question How can you follow a rule to complete an addition or subtraction function table?

Model and Draw

The rule for some tables is to add. For other tables the rule is to subtract.

Add 1	
2	3
4	
6	
8	

Subtract 1	
2	1
4	
6	
8	

Share and Show

Follow a rule to complete the table.

1.

Add 2	
10	
9	
8	
7	

2.

Subtract 2	
10	
9	
8	
7	

3.

Subtract 1	
3	
4	
7	
9	

Math Talk   What is the rule for the pattern in Exercise 1?

Getting Ready for Grade 2

On Your Own

Follow a rule to complete the table.

4.

Add 5	
7	
8	
9	
10	

5.

Subtract 5	
7	
8	
9	
10	

6.

Subtract 1	
8	
9	
11	
13	

7.

Subtract 3	
5	
7	
9	
11	

8.

Add 4	
6	
7	
8	
9	

9.

Add 6	
9	
8	
7	
6	

Problem Solving

10. Find the rule. Complete the table.

3	
	8
7	10
	12

TAKE HOME ACTIVITY • Copy the table for Exercise 9.
Change the rule to Subtract 3. Have your child complete the table.

Add 3 Numbers

Essential Question How can you choose a strategy to help add 3 numbers?

Model and Draw

When you add 3 numbers, you can add in any order.
Using a strategy can help.

Make a 10.

$$\begin{array}{r} 2 \\ 6 \\ +8 \\ \hline 16 \end{array} \quad \begin{array}{r} 10 \\ +6 \end{array}$$

Use doubles.

$$\begin{array}{r} 8 \\ 8 \\ +4 \\ \hline 20 \end{array} \quad \begin{array}{r} 16 \\ +4 \end{array}$$

Use count on.

$$\begin{array}{r} 6 \\ 8 \\ +3 \\ \hline 17 \end{array} \quad \begin{array}{r} 9 \\ +8 \end{array}$$

Share and Show

Use strategies to find the sums. Circle any strategy you use.

I.	$\begin{array}{r}4\\7\\+7\\\hline\end{array}$ make a 10 doubles count on	**2.**	$\begin{array}{r}9\\8\\+1\\\hline\end{array}$ make a 10 doubles count on	**3.**	$\begin{array}{r}4\\6\\+2\\\hline\end{array}$ make a 10 doubles count on
4.	$\begin{array}{r}8\\4\\+2\\\hline\end{array}$ make a 10 doubles count on	**5.**	$\begin{array}{r}6\\3\\+6\\\hline\end{array}$ make a 10 doubles count on	**6.**	$\begin{array}{r}6\\7\\+4\\\hline\end{array}$ make a 10 doubles count on

Math Talk Explain why you used the make a 10 strategy to solve Exercise 6.

On Your Own

Use a strategy to find the sum. Circle the
strategy you choose.

7.
$\begin{array}{r} 5 \\ 5 \\ +\ 5 \end{array}$ make a 10
doubles
count on

8.
$\begin{array}{r} 7 \\ 3 \\ +\ 5 \end{array}$ make a 10
doubles
count on

9.
$\begin{array}{r} 3 \\ 8 \\ +\ 8 \end{array}$ make a 10
doubles
count on

10.
$\begin{array}{r} 4 \\ 2 \\ +\ 7 \end{array}$ make a 10
doubles
count on

11.
$\begin{array}{r} 2 \\ 9 \\ +\ 2 \end{array}$ make a 10
doubles
count on

12.
$\begin{array}{r} 9 \\ 9 \\ +\ 1 \end{array}$ make a 10
doubles
count on

13.
$\begin{array}{r} 9 \\ 2 \\ +\ 8 \end{array}$ make a 10
doubles
count on

14.
$\begin{array}{r} 6 \\ 3 \\ +\ 7 \end{array}$ make a 10
doubles
count on

15.
$\begin{array}{r} 8 \\ 4 \\ +\ 1 \end{array}$ make a 10
doubles
count on

Problem Solving

16. Christine has 7 red buttons,
3 blue buttons, and 4 yellow
buttons. How many buttons
does she have?

_____ buttons

TAKE HOME ACTIVITY • Ask your child to choose 3 numbers from 1 to 9.
Have your child add to find the sum.

© Houghton Mifflin Harcourt Publishing Company

Add a One-Digit Number to a Two-Digit Number

Essential Question How can you find the sum of a 1-digit number and a 2-digit number?

Model and Draw

What is 54 + 2?

To find the sum, find how many **tens** and **ones** in all.

5 tens	**4** ones	**5 4**
+	**2** ones	+ **2**
5 tens	**6** ones	**5 6**

Share and Show

Add. Write the sum.

1. 72
    $+ 3$

2. 24
    $+ 1$

3. 41
    $+ 4$

4. 56
    $+ 2$

5. 14
    $+ 4$

6. 33
    $+ 6$

7. 61
    $+ 8$

8. 93
    $+ 4$

9. 31
    $+ 6$

10. 11
    $+ 7$

11. 40
    $+ 4$

12. 35
    $+ 3$

Math Talk How did you find the total number of ones in
Exercise 1?

On Your Own

Add. Write the sum.

13.
$$\begin{array}{r} 22 \\ + 7 \\ \hline \end{array}$$

14.
$$\begin{array}{r} 53 \\ + 3 \\ \hline \end{array}$$

15.
$$\begin{array}{r} 46 \\ + 2 \\ \hline \end{array}$$

16.
$$\begin{array}{r} 71 \\ + 8 \\ \hline \end{array}$$

17.
$$\begin{array}{r} 84 \\ + 5 \\ \hline \end{array}$$

18.
$$\begin{array}{r} 93 \\ + 4 \\ \hline \end{array}$$

19.
$$\begin{array}{r} 16 \\ + 3 \\ \hline \end{array}$$

20.
$$\begin{array}{r} 37 \\ + 1 \\ \hline \end{array}$$

21.
$$\begin{array}{r} 62 \\ + 2 \\ \hline \end{array}$$

22.
$$\begin{array}{r} 23 \\ + 5 \\ \hline \end{array}$$

23.
$$\begin{array}{r} 82 \\ + 2 \\ \hline \end{array}$$

24.
$$\begin{array}{r} 44 \\ + 4 \\ \hline \end{array}$$

Problem Solving

25. There are 23 children in the first grade class. Then 3 more children join the class. How many children are there now?

_____ children

TAKE HOME ACTIVITY • Tell your child you had 12 pennies and then you got 5 more. Have your child add to find how many pennies in all.

Add Two-Digit Numbers

Essential Question How can you find the sum of
two 2-digit numbers?

Model and Draw

What is 23 + 14?

You can find how many **tens** and **ones** in all.

2 tens	**3** ones		**2 3**
+ 1 ten	**4** ones		**+ 1 4**
_3_ tens	_7_ ones		$\boxed{3\,7}$

Share and Show

Add. Write the sum.

1. 82
  + 12

2. 25
  + 43

3. 15
  + 14

4. 71
  + 12

5. 36
  + 21

6. 43
  + 41

7. 57
  + 32

8. 21
  + 12

9. 12
  + 12

10. 41
  + 21

11. 32
  + 41

12. 51
  + 14

Math Talk   How many tens are in 26 + 11?
How do you know?

On Your Own

Add. Write the sum.

13. $\begin{array}{r} 83 \\ +12 \end{array}$	14. $\begin{array}{r} 73 \\ +21 \end{array}$	15. $\begin{array}{r} 16 \\ +51 \end{array}$	16. $\begin{array}{r} 23 \\ +43 \end{array}$
17. $\begin{array}{r} 24 \\ +55 \end{array}$	18. $\begin{array}{r} 67 \\ +21 \end{array}$	19. $\begin{array}{r} 64 \\ +23 \end{array}$	20. $\begin{array}{r} 51 \\ +24 \end{array}$
21. $\begin{array}{r} 26 \\ +32 \end{array}$	22. $\begin{array}{r} 51 \\ +25 \end{array}$	23. $\begin{array}{r} 46 \\ +22 \end{array}$	24. $\begin{array}{r} 34 \\ +45 \end{array}$

Problem Solving

25. Emma has 21 hair clips.
Her sister has 11 hair clips.
How many hair clips do
the girls have together?

_____ hair clips

TAKE HOME ACTIVITY • Tell your child you drove 21 miles and then you drove 16 more. Have your child add to find how many miles in all.

© Houghton Mifflin Harcourt Publishing Company

Repeated Addition

Essential Question How can you find how many items there are in equal groups without counting one at a time?

Model and Draw

When all groups have the same number they are equal groups.

Ayita is putting 2 plants on each step up to her porch. She has 4 steps. How many plants does she need?

There are 4 equal groups. There are 2 in each group. Add to find how many in all.

$\underline{2} + \underline{2} + \underline{2} + \underline{2} = \underline{8}$

Ayita needs $\underline{8}$ plants.

Share and Show

Use your MathBoard and ⬤. Make equal groups. Complete the addition sentence.

	Number of Equal Groups	Number in Each Group	How many in all?
1.	4	3	___ + ___ + ___ + ___ = ___
2.	2	5	___ + ___ = ___
3.	3	4	___ + ___ + ___ = ___

Math Talk How can you use addition to find 5 groups of 4?

Use your MathBoard and ⬤. Make equal groups. Complete the addition sentence.

	Number of Equal Groups	Number in Each Group	How many in all?
4.	2	3	____ + ____ = ____
5.	3	5	____ + ____ + ____ = ____
6.	4	4	____ + ____ + ____ + ____ = ____
7.	4	5	____ + ____ + ____ + ____ = ____
8.	5	7	____ + ____ + ____ + ____ + ____ = ____

Problem Solving Real World

Solve.

9. There are 3 flower pots. There are 2 flowers in each flower pot. How many flowers are there?

____ flowers

10. There are 2 plants. There are 4 leaves on each plant. How many leaves are there?

____ leaves

TAKE HOME ACTIVITY • Use dry cereal or pasta to make 3 equal groups of 5. Ask your child to find the total number of items.

© Houghton Mifflin Harcourt Publishing Company

Use Repeated Addition to Solve Problems

Essential Question How can you use repeated addition to solve problems?

 Model and Draw

Dyanna will have 3 friends at her party.
She wants to give each friend 4 balloons.
How many balloons does Dyanna need?

__12__ balloons

THINK $4 + 4 + 4 = 12$

Share and Show MATH BOARD

Draw pictures to show the story.
Write the addition sentence to solve.

1. Ted plays with 2 friends. He wants to give each friend 5 cards. How many cards does Ted need?

____ cards

2. Aisha shops with 4 friends. She wants to buy each friend 2 roses. How many roses does Aisha need?

____ roses

 **Math Talk** What pattern can you use to find the answer to Exercise 2?

© Houghton Mifflin Harcourt Publishing Company

Draw pictures to show the story.
Write the addition sentence to solve.

3. Lea plays with 3 friends. She wants to give each friend 5 ribbons. How many ribbons does Lea need?

_____ ribbons

4. Harry shops with 5 friends. He wants to buy each friend 2 pens. How many pens does Harry need?

_____ pens

5. Cam plays with 4 friends. She wants to give each friend 4 stickers. How many stickers does Cam need?

_____ stickers

Problem Solving

Circle the way you can model the problem. Then solve.

6. There are 4 friends. Each friend has 3 apples. How many apples are there?

4 groups of 4 apples

4 groups of 3 apples

3 groups of 4 apples

There are _____ apples.

TAKE HOME ACTIVITY • Use small items such as cereal pieces to act out each problem. Have your child check the answers on this page.

Name _____

✓ Checkpoint

Concepts and Skills

Follow the rule to complete each table.

1.

Add 3	
2	
4	
6	
8	

2.

Subtract 7	
10	
12	
13	
14	

3.

Add 6	
10	
9	
8	
7	

4.

Subtract 6	
15	
14	
13	
12	

Use strategies to find the sums. Circle any strategy you use.

5.
$$
\begin{array}{r}
4 \\
3 \\
+\ 4 \\
\hline
\end{array}
$$
make a 10
doubles
count on

6.
$$
\begin{array}{r}
3 \\
7 \\
+\ 5 \\
\hline
\end{array}
$$
make a 10
doubles
count on

Add. Write the sum.

7.
$$
\begin{array}{r}
32 \\
+\ 14 \\
\hline
\end{array}
$$

8.
$$
\begin{array}{r}
52 \\
+\ 46 \\
\hline
\end{array}
$$

9.
$$
\begin{array}{r}
18 \\
+\ 21 \\
\hline
\end{array}
$$

10.
$$
\begin{array}{r}
43 \\
+\ 35 \\
\hline
\end{array}
$$

Use your MathBoard and ●. Make equal groups.
Complete the addition sentence.

	Number of Equal Groups	Number in Each Group	How many in all?
11.	3	2	___ + ___ + ___ = ___
12.	2	4	___ + ___ = ___

13. Choose the way to model the problem.
James has 4 letters. He puts 2 stamps on each letter.
How many stamps does he use in all?

○ 2 groups of 4 stamps   ○ 4 groups of 4 stamps

○ 2 groups of 2 stamps   ○ 4 groups of 2 stamps

Name _____

Choose a Nonstandard Unit to Measure Length

Essential Question How can you decide which nonstandard unit to use to measure the length of an object?

Model and Draw

Use ⊂▭ to measure short things.

Use ✏️ to measure long things.

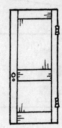

Share and Show

MATH BOARD

Use real objects. Circle the unit you would use to measure. Then measure.

	Object	Unit	Measurement
1.		⊂▭ ✏️	about ____
2.		⊂▭ ✏️	about ____
3.		⊂▭ ✏️	about ____
4.		⊂▭ ✏️	about ____

Math Talk Alex measured a book with ⊂▭. Then he measured with ✏️. Did he use more ⊂▭ or ✏️? Explain.

two hundred fifty-three **P253**

On Your Own

Use real objects. Choose a unit to measure the length. Circle it. Then measure.

	Object	Unit	Measurement
5.			about _____
6.			about _____
7.			about _____
8.			about _____

Problem Solving · Real World

9. Fred uses to measure the stick.
Sue measures the stick and gets the same measurement.
Circle the unit that Sue uses.

 TAKE HOME ACTIVITY • Have your child measure something around the house by using small objects such as paper clips and then by using larger objects such as pencils. Discuss why the measurements differ.

Name _____

Use a Non-Standard Ruler

Essential Question How can you use a non-standard measuring tool to find length?

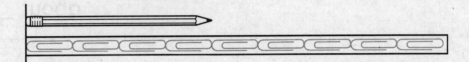
Model and Draw

About how long is the pencil?

The end of the pencil and the end of the ⚲ must line up. Count how many ⚲ from one end of the pencil to the other.

about __4__ ⚲

Share and Show MATH BOARD

About how long is the string?

1.

about ____ ⚲

2.

about ____ ⚲

Math Talk In Exercise 1, why must the end of the pencil and the end of the ⚲ line up?

Getting Ready for Grade 2 two hundred fifty-five **P255**

On Your Own

About how long is the string?

3.

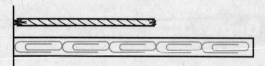

about ____ ⬭

4.

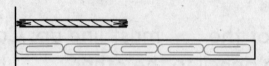

about ____ ⬭

5.

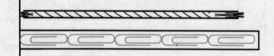

about ____ ⬭

Problem Solving (Real World)

6. Wendy measures her pencil. She says it is about 2 ⬭ long. Is she correct? Explain.

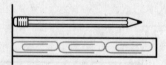

_____

_____

Name _____

Compare Lengths

Essential Question How can you compare lengths of objects?

Model and Draw

First, write 1, 2, and 3 to order the strings from **shortest** to **longest**.

Then measure with ⬜.

1 | strings

about __4__ ⬜ ← Shortest

3 | strings

about __8__ ⬜ ← Longest

2 | strings

about __6__ ⬜

Share and Show

MATH BOARD

Write 1, 2, and 3 to order the strings from **shortest** to **longest**. Then measure with ⬜. Write the lengths.

1. ___ | strings

about ____ ⬜

___ | strings

about ____ ⬜

___ | strings

about ____ ⬜

Math Talk How can measuring with cubes tell you the order of the strings?

Getting Ready for Grade 2

2. Write I, 2, and 3 to order the strings from **shortest** to **longest**. Then measure with ⬚. Write the lengths.

—— about ____ ⬚

—— about ____ ⬚

—— about ____ ⬚

3. Write I, 2, and 3 to order the strings from **shortest** to **longest**. Then measure with ⬚. Write the lengths.

—— about ____ ⬚

—— about ____ ⬚

—— about ____ ⬚

Problem Solving *Real World*

4. Kate has these ribbons. Kate gives Hannah the longest one. Measure with ⬚ and write the length of Hannah's ribbon.

about ____ ⬚

TAKE HOME ACTIVITY • Give your child three strips of paper. Have your child cut them about 4 paper clips long, about 2 paper clips long, and about 5 paper clips long. Then have your child order the paper strips from shortest to longest.

Name _____

Time to the Hour and Half Hour

Essential Question How do you tell time to the hour and half hour on an analog clock?

Model and Draw

The hour hand and the minute hand show the time.
Write the time shown on the clock.

4:00

4:30

Share and Show

Read the clock. Write the time.

1.

_____

2.

_____

3.

_____

Math Talk   Why does the hour hand point halfway
between 5 and 6 at half past 5:00?

On Your Own

Read the clock. Write the time.

4.

_____

5.

_____

6.

_____

7.

_____

8.

_____

9.

_____

Problem Solving Real World

Draw and write to show the time.

10. Liam has soccer practice at half past 10:00.

_____

TAKE HOME ACTIVITY • Say a time, such as half past 1:00 or 7:00. Ask your child where the clock hands will point at that time.

✓ Checkpoint

Concepts and Skills

Use real objects. Choose a unit to measure the length.
Then measure.

Object	Unit	Measurement
I.	⬭ ▪	about ____
2.	⬭ ▪	about ____
3. MATH	⬭ ▪	about ____

How long is the yarn? Use the star ruler to measure.

4.

____ stars long

5.

____ stars long

© Houghton Mifflin Harcourt Publishing Company

Write 1, 2, and 3 to measure the
strings from **shortest** to **longest.**
Then measure with cubes. Write the lengths.

6.

_____   _____ cubes long

_____   _____ cubes long

_____   _____ cubes long

7.

_____   _____ cubes long

_____   _____ cubes long

_____   _____ cubes long

8. Read the clock. Choose the correct time.

○   8:00

○   8:30

○   9:00

○   9:30

Name _____

Use a Picture Graph
Essential Question How do you read a picture graph?

Model and Draw

Our Favorite Hot Dog Toppings					
🧂 mustard	⚲	⚲	⚲		
🍾 ketchup	⚲	⚲	⚲	⚲	⚲

Each ⚲ stands for 1 child.

__3__ children chose 🧂.

Most children chose __ketchup__.

__2__ fewer children chose 🧂 than 🍾.

Share and Show

Our Sock Colors						
🧦 black	⚲	⚲				
🧦 white	⚲	⚲	⚲	⚲	⚲	⚲
🧦 blue	⚲	⚲	⚲			

Each ⚲ stands for 1 child.

Use the picture graph to answer the questions.

1. How many children are wearing 🧦? _____

2. What color of socks are most of the children wearing? _____

3. How many more children wear 🧦 than 🧦? _____

Math Talk   How did you find the answer to Exercise 3?

Getting Ready for Grade 2

two hundred sixty-three **P263**

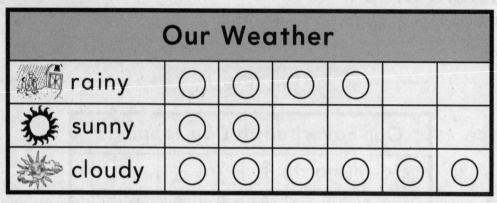

Our Weather

rainy	○	○	○	○	
sunny	○	○			
cloudy	○	○	○	○	○ ○

Each ○ stands for 1 day.

Use the picture graph to answer each question.

4. How many days in all are shown on the graph?

_____ days

5. What was the weather for most days? Circle.

6. How many fewer days were 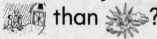 than ☁?

_____ days

7. How many ☀ and ☁ days were there?

_____ days

8. Today is sunny. Robin puts one more ☀ on the graph. How many ☀ days are there now?

_____ days

 TAKE HOME ACTIVITY • Help your child make a picture graph to show the eye color of 10 friends and family members.

Name _____

Use a Bar Graph

Essential Question How do you read a bar graph?

Model and Draw

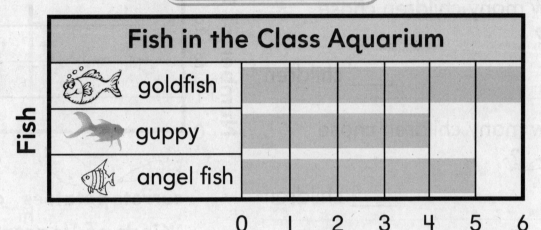

Fish in the Class Aquarium

Fish		0	1	2	3	4	5	6
	goldfish							
	guppy							
	angel fish							

Number of Fish

To find how many, read the number below the end of the bar.

___6___ fish are 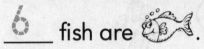.

Share and Show

MATH BOARD

Use the bar graph to answer the questions.

1. How many fish are in the aquarium?

____ fish

2. How many fish in the aquarium are ?

____ fish

3. How many fewer fish are than ?

____ fish

4. Are more of the fish or ?

_____

 Math Talk How did you find the answer for Exercise 1?

Use the bar graph to answer the questions.

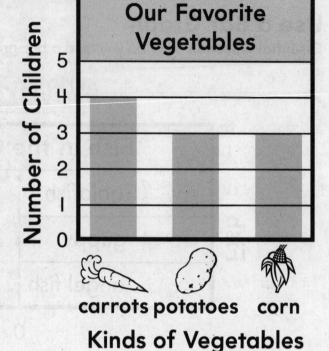

Our Favorite Vegetables

Number of Children

carrots potatoes corn

Kinds of Vegetables

5. How many children chose 🥔?

_____ children

6. How many children chose 🥕?

_____ children

7. Which vegetable did most children choose? Circle.

8. Which vegetables were chosen the same number of times? Circle.

Problem Solving Real World

Use the bar graph to solve.

9. Brad and Glen both like corn the best. If the boys add this to the graph, how many children will have chosen corn?

_____ children

 TAKE HOME ACTIVITY • Ask your child to decide whether they prefer carrots or potatoes. Then have your child color to add their choice to the bar graph on this page.

Take a Survey

Essential Question How can you take a survey?

Model and Draw

You can take a **survey** to get information. Jane took a survey of her friends' favorite wild animals. The tally chart shows the results.

Favorite Wild Animal	
Animal	**Tally**
elephant	卌I
monkey	III
tiger	II

REMEMBER
Each tally mark stands for one friend's choice.

Share and Show

1. Take a survey.
   Ask 10 classmates which wild animal is their favorite. Use tally marks to show their answers.

Our Favorite Wild Animal	
Animal	**Tally**
elephant	
monkey	
tiger	

_____

2. How many children did not choose tiger?

   _____ children

_____

3. Did more children choose elephant or tiger? _____

_____

4. The most children chose
   _____ as their favorite.

Math Talk   Describe a different survey that you could take. What would the choices be?

5. Take a survey. Ask 10 classmates which color is their favorite. Use tally marks to show their answers.

Our Favorite Color	
Color	Tally
red	
blue	
green	

6. Which color was chosen by the fewest classmates? _____

7. Which color did the most classmates choose? _____

8. Did more classmates choose red or green? _____

9. _____ classmates chose a color that was not red.

10. Did fewer children choose blue or green? _____

Problem Solving

11. Jeff wants to ask 10 classmates which snack is their favorite. He makes 1 tally mark for each child's answer. How many more classmates does he need to ask?

Our Favorite Snack	
Snack	Tally
pretzels	II
apples	I
popcorn	₩

_____ more classmates

 TAKE HOME ACTIVITY • Have your child survey family members about their favorite sport and make a tally chart to show the results.

Identify Shapes

Essential Question How can attributes help you identify a shape?

Model and Draw

The number of sides and vertices help you identify a shape.

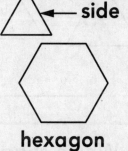
← vertex
← side

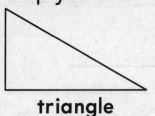 triangle

 square

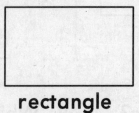 rectangle

 trapezoid

hexagon

3 sides, 3 vertices   4 sides, 4 vertices   6 sides, 6 vertices

Share and Show

 MATH BOARD

Circle to answer the question. Write to name the shape.

1. Which shape has 4 sides?

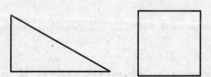

_____

2. Which shape has 3 vertices?

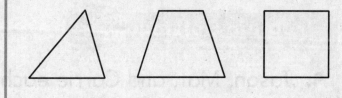

_____

3. Which shape has 6 sides?

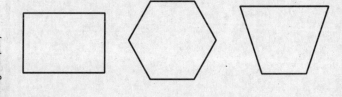

_____

4. Which shape has 4 vertices?

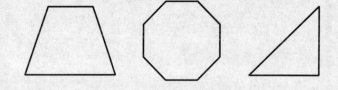

_____

Math Talk   How are a square and a rectangle alike?

Circle to answer the question. Write to name the shape.

5. Which shape has 3 sides?

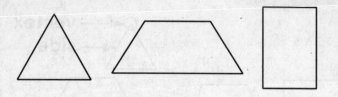

_____

6. Which shape has 4 vertices?

_____

7. Which shape has 4 sides?

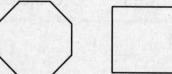
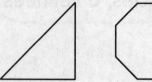

_____

8. Which shape has 6 vertices?

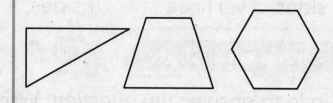

_____

Problem Solving Real World

9. Jason, Mat, and Carrie each draw a shape with 4 sides. The shapes look different and have different names.

Draw 3 shapes the children might have drawn. Write to name each shape.

_____   _____   _____

TAKE HOME ACTIVITY • Have your child look around the house to find something that looks like a rectangle. Then have your child point to the rectangle and count the vertices. Repeat with the sides.

Equal Shares

Essential Question How can you name two or four equal shares?

Model and Draw

half	half

___2___ equal shares

___2___ halves

fourth	fourth
fourth	fourth

___4___ equal shares

___4___ fourths

Share and Show

Circle the shape that shows equal shares. Write to name the equal shares.

1.

_____

2.
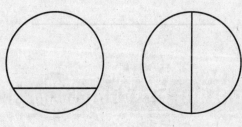

_____

3.

_____

4.

_____

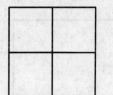 **Math Talk** Are all equal shares the same size and shape? Explain.

Circle the shape that shows equal shares. Write to name the equal shares.

5.

_____

6.
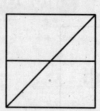
_____

7.
 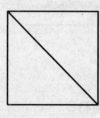
_____

8.
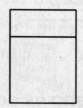 
_____

Problem Solving Real World

9. Riley wants to share his cracker with a friend. Draw to show two different ways Riley can cut the cracker into equal shares.

 TAKE HOME ACTIVITY • Ask your child to help you cut a piece of toast into fourths.

Name _____

✓ Checkpoint

Concepts and Skills

Use the picture graph to answer Exercises 1 and 2.

Our Favorite Fruit								
🍎 apple	👤	👤	👤	👤	👤			
🍌 banana	👤	👤	👤	👤	👤	👤	👤	👤
🍊 orange	👤	👤	👤					

Each 👤 stands for 1 child.

1. How many children choose an orange? _____

2. Which fruit was chosen most often? _____

- -

Use the bar graph to answer Exercises 3 and 4.

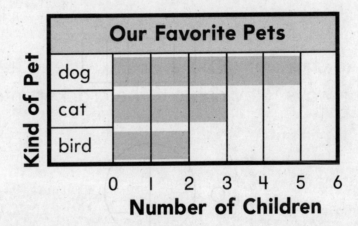

3. Which pet did most children choose? _____

4. How many more children chose a cat than a bird?

_____

5. Take a survey. Ask 8 classmates which sport is their favorite. Use tally marks to show their answers.

Our Favorite Sport	
Sport	**Tally**
baseball	
football	
soccer	

6. Did more children choose baseball or soccer? _____

Circle to answer the question. Then write the shape name.

7. Which shape has 4 vertices?

_____

8. Which shape shows fourths?

○ 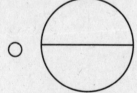   ○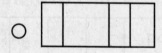

○ 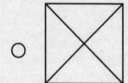   ○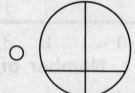